EIGHT WAYS

THE ARTISTRY OF TEACHING WITH MULTIPLE INTELLIGENCES

David Lazear

OF TEACHING

SkyLight
PROFESSIONAL DEVELOPMENT
Arlington Heights, Illinois

Eight Ways of Teaching: The Artistry of Teaching with Multiple Intelligences
Third Edition

Published by SkyLight Professional Development
2626 S. Clearbrook Dr., Arlington Heights, IL 60005
800-348-4474 or 847-290-6600
Fax 847-290-6609
info@kylightedu.com
http://www.skylightedu.com

Senior Vice President, Product Development: Robin Fogarty
Manager, Product Development: Ela Aktay
Editor: Heidi Ray
Book Designer: Bruce Leckie
Cover Designer and Illustrator: David Stockman
Production Coordination: Bob Crump

LCCCN 98-61254
ISBN 1-57517-119-8

2332McN
Item Number 1668

ZYXWVUTSRQPONMLKJIHGFEDCB
06 05 04 03 02 01 00   20 19 18 17 16 15

Table of Contents

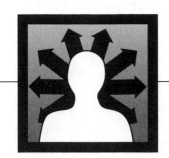

Foreword

In 1967, a Harvard study of how artistic knowledge develops and functions was begun. At this time Howard Gardner and David Perkins, currently the project's codirectors, were first-year graduate students. In 1981, Howard Gardner was awarded a MacArthur Prize to fund a shift to an educational emphasis in the work of Project Zero. In the APA Monitor article about the award, the author noted that "early in his career, Gardner had been a committed Piagetian, but as he pursued his own studies, Gardner came to view Piaget's theories as too narrow a notion of how the human mind works." In 1980, *The Mind's New Science* was conceived and supported by the Sloan Foundation.

Gardner was already formulating his multiple intelligences theory based on his belief that there is not just one form of cognition which cuts across all human thinking. His theory proposed that there are multiple intelligences with autonomous intelligence capacities. A book was forming in his mind in the late 1970s, and through a large grant from the Bernard Van Leer Foundation, he began to write *Frames of Mind,* which he described as a "contemporary, empirically-based effort to answer long-standing philosophical questions about Psychology's theoretical underpinnings!"

Frames of Mind was published in 1983. In 1984, Howard Gardner presented his new theory to a large number of educators who attended The Coming Education Explosion conference at the Tarrytown Conference Center in New York. The conference program was packed with leading-edge educational theorists and practitioners—all of whom were finding successful, innovative ways to foster learning and human development. As soon as Gardner spoke, it became clear that his theory provided a framework for all of the other presentations. The implications for education at all levels and in every setting were evident.

That conference touched off a wave of educational innovation throughout the country, and was the beginning of a series of seven international conferences that New Horizons for Learning produced with the multiple intelligences theory as a framework. Each of those conferences presented information through many kinds of intelligences in a specially created environment filled with music, colorful mind maps created as the presenters spoke, exercises and other physical activities at every break, and dancing into the night.

Attendees reported that they were able to absorb more information than they ever thought possible, and, moreover, during the conference, rather than being tired, they became energized. After each of these events, teachers and school administrators could hardly wait to go back to their classrooms and schools to apply what they had learned. And from many different parts of the country letters poured in with enthusiastic reports about students who were learning in new ways, about new curriculum being designed, and about classrooms and schools taking on a new look.

In 1984, eight Indianapolis public school teachers submitted a proposal to the Indiana Department of Education for a grant to plan a curriculum for the creatively gifted and talented. During the next school year the teachers met on a voluntary basis to complete their project, and in 1985 they approached the superintendent to ask for their own school. That fall they met with Howard Gardner in order to share the results of their work based on his multiple intelligences theory and to discuss their plans to develop their own school built around the theory. The "Indianapolis Eight" set up a steering committee of experts to advise them, and by 1986 they submitted their proposal to begin the Key School, which opened its doors the next year.

As one of the first schools to be based on the multiple intelligences theory, the Key School, under the leadership of Pat Bolanos, has pioneered the classroom application of Gardner's work, including new kinds of teaching and learning, evaluation, and expanded possibilities for human development.

Also in 1987, Thomas Armstrong, a psychologist and learning specialist, wrote *In Their Own Way,* an important parenting guide based on Gardner's theory. Armstrong's book helps parents and teachers to understand the complex differences among children and how to create a stimulating and nurturing environment to foster the development of all their intelligences. It has done much to further the understanding and appreciation of an expanded view of intelligence.

During the last few years, a large number of new multiple intelligences programs have been springing up not only in the United States but throughout the world. Following are but a few examples:

Bruce Campbell, a third/fourth grade teacher in the Marysville, Washington School district, has set up multiple intelligences stations in his classroom so his students learn everything in eight different ways. As a result, his students not only have improved academically, but also exhibit improved behavior, diverse learning and thinking skills, and the ability to work in both cooperative and self-directed ways. His work has been so successful that it has gained national attention.

Linda MacRae Campbell has trained thousands of teachers in multiple intelligences theory in school districts throughout this country and abroad. She created and directs a teacher certification program at Antioch University in Seattle with this theory at the heart of the program. This program has been recognized as one of the most innovative in the country.

In inner-city Chicago, the Guggenheim School has been implementing accelerated learning techniques and multiple intelligences theory for the last six years. A visionary principal and dedicated teachers trained in multisensory teaching strategies moved the school from seventeenth place out of seventeen schools in the district to first place in one year.

The New City School in Saint Louis, Missouri has studied multiple intelligences theory for two years and is now in its first year of implementation with exciting results in every classroom.

Seven Oaks Elementary School in Lacey, Washington has hired a specialist in each of the eight intelligences as the school embarks on its first year of applying multiple intelligences theory to teaching and learning.

The Renaissance Project, codirected by Dr. David Thornburg (director of the Thornburg Center for Professional Development) and Sue Teele (director of Education Extension at the University of California, Riverside), is a research project that links instructional strategies and technology to multiple intelligences theory. The project is focused on developing teaching methods and authentic assessment measures to help students develop their capabilities in all of the intelligences.

In LaGrange, Illinois, Pat Gullett, who has taught high school art for twenty years, changed her whole approach to teaching as a result of her introduction to multiple intelligences theory. On completing her master's program in Interdisciplinary Arts Education at Columbia College she created an exhibit of seven mixed-media art pieces based on multiple intelligences theory. The exhibit covered a thirty-foot wall.

And New Horizons for Learning has continued to disseminate information on successful practices of multiple intelligences theory and practice through its newsletter, seminars, and conferences offered throughout the United States, the former Soviet Union, Europe, and Central and South America.

It is into this context of pioneering efforts in education that David Lazear offers his comprehensive book of teaching and learning strategies to further expand the practical application of the theory of multiple intelligences. Over the years, growing numbers of educators have become eager to explore the possibilities of helping their students to expand their capacities more fully by implementing multiple intelligences theory in their schools. *Eight Ways of Teaching* will offer them useful, creative, and stimulating strategies to vitalize their classrooms and help their students learn in exciting new ways.

The format of this book is also appropriate to multiple intelligences theory, with attractive and informative illustrations, charts, and diagrams and many activities to apply in the teaching of all subjects. It is noteworthy that in each section Lazear has made sure to include suggestions on the teaching of transfer, which does not automatically occur in most subjects. Making sure that students can apply what they have learned in contexts outside of the classroom is of major importance in making learning relevant and of long-lasting value.

Lazear has also included specific examples of authentic assessment that go far beyond what standardized tests are capable of revealing. Portfolios of student work, student projects, and journals are not only useful measures of student progress, but offer students insights about their own work. Furthermore, they provide rich opportunities for students to engage in reflective thinking that is often neglected by teachers in their haste to cover more subject matter.

Every teacher will find numerous examples of how to motivate students, present material in a variety of ways, and offer opportunities for practical and creative application of what has been learned. *Eight Ways of Teaching* is a fine handbook for teaching and learning in today's world.

Dee Dickinson
President, New Horizons for Learning, 1991

Preface

My interest in the theory of multiple intelligences and its application in the classroom comes from a number of experiences, one of which is having mentored two daughters through grade school and junior high. Two events stand out in my mind as I begin this companion volume to my first book on this subject, *Eight Ways of Knowing: Teaching for Multiple Intelligences.*

The first experience was an encounter with my youngest daughter's fifth-grade teacher. Naomi was having difficulties in a number of subjects, mostly those in which understanding the relationships of ideas, events, and people were important (history, social studies, literature, and the like). In a parent-teacher meeting the teacher explained that Naomi simply didn't have the capacity for grasping complex relationships and intricacy of detail and that she probably needed to be placed in a lower-level class.

Almost in the same breath the teacher pointed to a piece of Naomi's artwork on the wall. It was near Valentine's Day and she had created a large heart poster. It looked like a simple valentine with lace decorations. But as I got closer I discovered that she had created a multilayered, three-dimensional heart from construction paper that had hearts within hearts within hearts all forming an intricate maze of pathways to a central heart chamber where, in raised, multicolored letters, made from hundreds of miniature hearts (much like the flower petals on floats in the Rose Parade), she had created the message Be mine, Valentine! I was stunned, especially in light of the fact that I had just been told that my daughter did not have the capacity for dealing with complex relationships and intricate detail!

Almost immediately I said to the teacher, as I pointed to the valentine on the wall, "If she could learn her history, social studies, and literature this way, she'd get it!" To which the teacher replied, "Mr. Lazear, art is art and history is history. History is not art. History involves learning facts, dates, people, and events and how they are all related. Your daughter isn't learning these things."

While I did not know then what I know now about multiple intelligences, I knew this teacher was wrong about the separateness of the disciplines. I, perhaps instinctively, knew that somehow Naomi's highly developed visual/spatial capacities could be tapped to help her with her studies. It was many years later that I discovered how.

The second experience involved my eldest daughter, Esther. Esther is very much a bodily/kinesthetic knower and learner. In fact, over the years many teachers have called me with what was supposed to be alarming news—that she was hyperactive. In any event, when she was in junior high school, she came home from school one day with a list of twenty vocabulary words to learn for a test the next day. I sent her to her room to memorize the words and to come back to me when she had learned them.

After a period of time she came to me and said, "Okay Daddy, I'm ready. Test me." I proceeded to do just that. She got less than fifty percent of the words right. So I said to her, "Esther, you're an intelligent girl. You're just not thinking. Back to your room and write each word and definition five times, and this time pay attention to what you are doing!" Reluctantly she wandered off to her room. After a reasonable amount of time, she brought her work to me and I was sure she would have them this time; after all, *I would have if it had been me*! I tested her again, and to my dismay, she had improved very little. Finally, totally exasperated, she said to me, "Daddy, I can't learn this way. I've got to be moving around. I've got to learn with my body!"

Well, for the next twenty to thirty minutes very strange and wonderful things transpired in my study. We proceeded to "embody" the meaning of the words—that is, learn them with our bodies. I would say the word and its definition and she would create body movements and physical gestures that somehow communicated the meaning of the word to her. We were crawling on the floor, leaping in the air, jumping off furniture, doing all manner of strange and bizarre things. But at the end of this time, to my amazement, she had the list down perfectly *with her body!* I would say the word, the word would remind her of the body movement, which she would then perform, and, the body movement helped trigger the verbal definition.

This book is dedicated to Esther and Naomi, and to all children in our schools who have other ways of knowing and learning than our current systems of education take into account. It is my hope that

SkyLight Training and Publishing Inc.

educators will use this book, and *Eight Ways of Knowing,* to begin a very important educational experiment in teaching *for, with,* and *about* multiple intelligences. I have called this book *Eight Ways of Teaching* in order to suggest that our instructional methods must undergo a revolution if we are to reach all students sitting in our classrooms, who have at least eight ways of knowing and probably many more! I often wonder how many kids are in special education classes simply because we have not known how to approach their knowing and learning through a different set of doorways than the verbal/linguistic and logical/mathematical, which dominate all systems of education in the Western world today. In a time when programs for the gifted flourish in many schools, I find myself an advocate for the giftedness of every child, if only we as teachers can find the keys to unlock their full potential.

David Lazear
Chicago, 1991

SkyLight Training and Publishing Inc.

Introduction

The Artistry of Teaching *for*, *With*, and *About* Multiple Intelligences

What is intelligence? How can we measure it? And once it's been measured, what should we do with it?

For many centuries humankind has been trying to understand the workings of the mind—sometimes through magic, sometimes through psychology, sometimes through sociology and anthropology, sometimes through religion, and sometimes through medicine. In the last thirty to fifty years, researchers from every walk of life, and from virtually every profession and academic discipline have begun a new set of explorations of a new frontier—the human mind and how it works. And they have been coming up with some astonishing discoveries, many of which have called into question all previous understandings about humanity and its potentials:

- **Right brain/left brain.** In 1981 Dr. Roger Sperry received a Nobel Peace Prize for his research into the different ways the left and right hemispheres of the brain process information. In the left hemisphere processing is more linear and sequential, while the right brain's processing tends to be more simultaneous and creative. These two modalities are brought together in a new area of research known as whole-brain processing.

- **Triune brain.** Dr. Paul MacLean, Chief of the Laboratory of Brain Evolution and Behavior at the National Institute of Mental Health in Washington, D.C., has done an important research study that suggests that within our one brain there are three separate brains that come from our earlier development as a species. As humans developed, and the need for more involved levels of thinking and mental processes were required, the brain simply grew new layers, each more complex and more intricate than its predecessor. While all three brains are still present in humans, they operate as a unified whole giving us the wisdom and potentials from our evolutionary past.

- **Intelligence can be enhanced and amplified.** In the past intelligence was viewed as a fixed, static entity. It was something you were born with and were stuck with for life. However, contemporary brain-mind researchers, such as Dr. Jean Houston, Dr. Robert Masters, Dr. Willis Harman, and Dr. Luis Machado, are suggesting that possibly the only limits to our intelligence are self-made and are related to our beliefs about what is possible. What is more, Israeli psychologist and researcher, Dr. Reuven Feuerstein, along with a number of others, suggest that at any age, and at almost any ability level, one's mental functioning can be improved. We can, apparently, all learn to be more intelligent by consciously activating perception and knowing on more levels than we usually use!

- **The brain is a like a hologram.** Dr. Karl Pribram of Stanford University has proposed a fascinating theory of the brain as a hologram. In a hologram, all of the basic information of the whole is stored within each part of the hologram, so that if it is in some way shattered, each piece contains and is capable of reproducing all of the information of the former whole. Pribram suggests that memory storage may work like this in the brain. Think for a moment about times when a very small fragment of a memory is able to bring back a full-sensory experience of something that may have happened in your childhood.

- **Intelligence is a multiple reality.** Dr. Howard Gardner and his team of Harvard researchers involved in Project Zero have postulated that there are many forms of intelligence—many ways by which we know, understand, and learn about our world—not just one. And most of these ways of knowing go beyond those that dominate Western culture and education, and they definitely go beyond what current IQ tests can measure. He proposed a schema of eight intelligences and suggests that there are probably many others that we have not yet been able to test!

It is the research of Howard Gardner on which this book, as well as *Eight Ways of Knowing,* is primarily based. Let me briefly summarize the eight intelligences Gardner identified:

Verbal/linguistic intelligence is responsible for the production of language and all the complex possibilities that follow, including poetry, humor, storytelling, grammar, metaphors, similes, abstract reasoning, symbolic thinking, conceptual patterning, reading, and writing. This intelligence can be seen in such people as poets, playwrights, storytellers, novelists, public speakers, and comedians.

Logical/mathematical intelligence is most often associated with what we call scientific thinking or inductive reasoning, although deductive thought processes are also involved. This intelligence involves the capacity to recognize patterns, work with abstract symbols (such as numbers and geometric shapes), and discern relationships and/or see connections between separate and distinct pieces of information. This intelligence can be seen in such people as scientists, computer programmers, accountants, lawyers, bankers, and of course, mathematicians.

The logical/mathematical and verbal/linguistic intelligences form the basis for most systems of Western education, as well as for all forms of currently existing standardized testing programs.

Visual spatial intelligence deals with the visual arts (including painting, drawing, and sculpting); navigation, mapmaking, and architecture (which involve the use of space and knowing how to get around in it); and games such as chess (which require the ability to visualize objects from different perspectives and angles). The key sensory base of this intelligence is the sense of sight, but also the ability to form mental images and pictures in the mind. This intelligence can be seen in such people as architects, graphic artists, cartographers, industrial design draftspersons, and of course, visual artists (painters and sculptors).

Bodily/kinesthetic intelligence is the ability to use the body to express emotion (as in dance and body language), to play a game (as in sports), and to create a new product (as in invention). Learning by doing has long been recognized as an important part of education. Our bodies know things our minds do not and cannot know in any other way. For example, our bodies know how to ride a bike, roller-skate, type, and parallel park a car. This intelligence can been seen in such people as actors, athletes, mimes, dancers, and inventors.

Musical/rhythmic intelligence includes such capacities as the recognition and use of rhythmic and tonal patterns, and sensitivity to sounds from the environment, the human voice, and musical instruments. Many of us learned the alphabet through this intelligence and the A-B-C song. Of all forms of intelligence, the consciousness altering effect of music and rhythm on the brain is probably the greatest. This intelligence can be seen in advertising professionals (those who write catchy jingles to sell a product), performance musicians, rock musicians, dance bands, composers, and music teachers.

Interpersonal intelligence involves the ability to work cooperatively with others in a group as well as the ability to communicate, verbally and nonverbally, with other people. It builds on the capacity to notice distinctions among others such as contrasts in moods, temperament, motivations, and intentions. In the more advanced forms of this intelligence, one can literally pass over into another's perspective and read his or her intentions and desires. One can have genuine empathy for another's feelings, fears, anticipations, and beliefs. This form of intelligence is usually highly developed in such people as counselors, teachers, therapists, politicians, and religious leaders.

Intrapersonal intelligence involves knowledge of the internal aspects of the self, such as knowledge of feelings, the range of emotional responses, thinking processes, self-reflection, and a sense of or intuition about spiritual realities. Intrapersonal intelligence allows us to be conscious of our consciousness; that is, to step back from ourselves and watch ourselves as an outside observer. It involves our capacity to experience wholeness and unity, to discern patterns of connection within the larger order of things, to perceive higher states of consciousness, to experience the lure of the future, and to dream of and actualize the possible. This intelligence can be seen in such people as philosophers, psychiatrists, spiritual counselors and gurus, and cognitive pattern researchers.

Naturalist intelligence involves the ability to discern, comprehend, and appreciate the various flora and fauna of the world of nature as opposed to the world created by human beings. It involves such capacities as recognizing and classifying species, growing plants and raising or taming animals, knowing how to appropriately use the natural world (e.g., living off the land), and having a curiosity about the natural world, its creatures, weather patterns, physical history, etc. In working with and developing the naturalist intelligence one often discovers a sense of wonder, awe, and respect for all the various phenomena and species (plant and animal) of the natural world. This intelligence can be seen in such people as farmers, hunters, zookeepers, gardeners, cooks, veterinarians, nature guides, and forest rangers.

On the following pages are a summary of the multiple intelligences (fig. 0.1) and the Multiple Intelligences Capacities Wheel (fig. 0.2). I created the wheel for *Eight Ways of Knowing* to show some of the specific capacities (what Gardner sometimes calls subintelligences) that are related to the eight ways of knowing.

SkyLight Training and Publishing Inc.

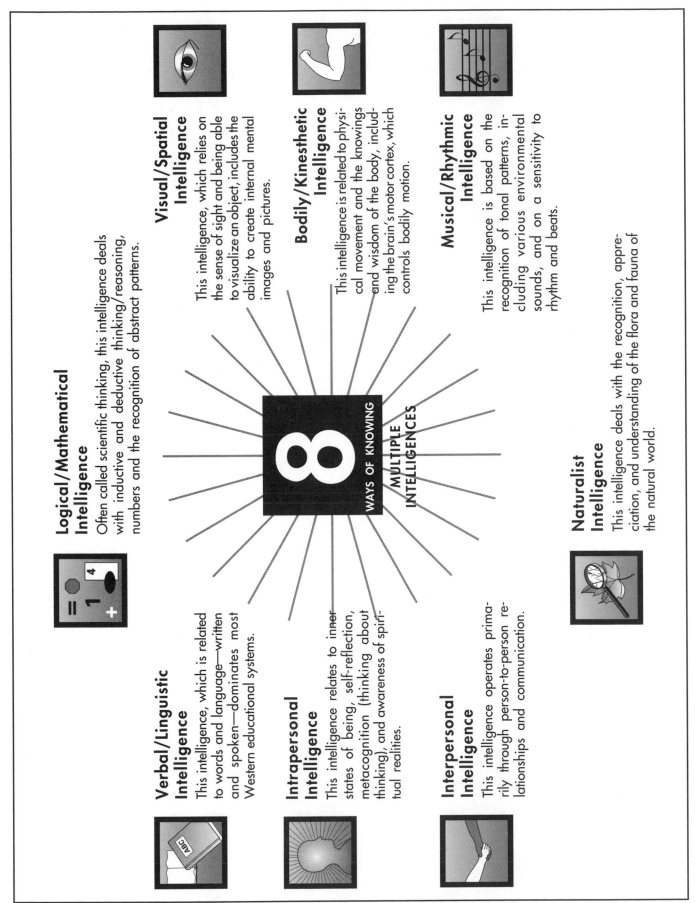

Figure 0.1

Logical/Mathematical Intelligence

Often called scientific thinking, this intelligence deals with inductive and deductive thinking/reasoning, numbers and the recognition of abstract patterns.

Visual/Spatial Intelligence

This intelligence, which relies on the sense of sight and being able to visualize an object, includes the ability to create internal mental images and pictures.

Bodily/Kinesthetic Intelligence

This intelligence is related to physical movement and the knowings and wisdom of the body, including the brain's motor cortex, which controls bodily motion.

Musical/Rhythmic Intelligence

This intelligence is based on the recognition of tonal patterns, including various environmental sounds, and on a sensitivity to rhythm and beats.

Verbal/Linguistic Intelligence

This intelligence, which is related to words and language—written and spoken—dominates most Western educational systems.

Intrapersonal Intelligence

This intelligence relates to inner states of being, self-reflection, metacognition (thinking about thinking), and awareness of spiritual realities.

Interpersonal Intelligence

This intelligence operates primarily through person-to-person relationships and communication.

Naturalist Intelligence

This intelligence deals with the recognition, appreciation, and understanding of the flora and fauna of the natural world.

8 WAYS OF KNOWING

MULTIPLE INTELLIGENCES

Multiple Intelligences Capacities Wheel

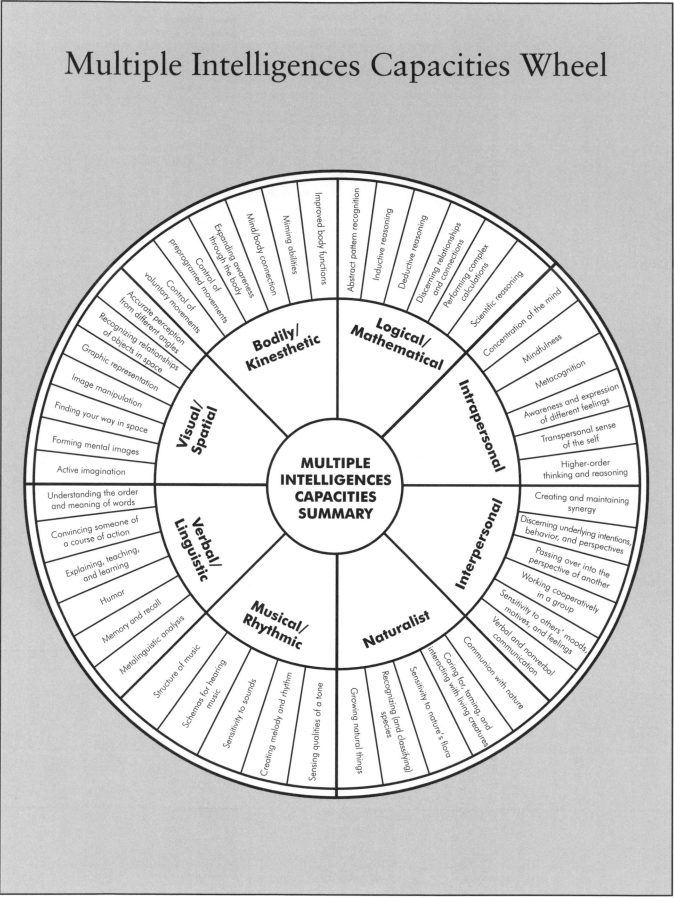

Figure 0.2

The good news is that each of us have all of these intelligences, but not all of them are developed equally and thus we do not know how to use them effectively. In fact, it is usually the case that one or two intelligences are stronger and more fully developed than the others. But, this need not be a permanent condition. *We have within ourselves the capacity to activate all of our intelligences!*

What are possibilities of teaching *for*, *with*, and *about* multiple intelligences in the classroom?

There are at least three different types of lessons that are needed:

1. **Intelligence as a subject unto itself** *(teaching* **for** *multiple intelligences).* Each of the intelligences can be taught as a subject in its own right: music skills, language, art as a formal discipline, mathematical calculation and reasoning, skillful body movement (as in physical education, dance, and drama), and various social skills necessary for effective functioning in our society. Teaching these subjects requires a grasp of the developmental stages of each intelligence as well as an understanding of the accumulated cultural wisdom on the subject, the formal knowledge base, and the practical methods, skills, and techniques of the intelligence.

2. **Intelligence as a means to acquire knowledge** *(teaching* **with** *multiple intelligences).* Each of the intelligences can be used as a means to gain knowledge in areas beyond itself: using body movement to learn vocabulary words, music to teach math concepts, art (drawing, painting, and sculpture) to bring to life different periods of history and different cultures, debate to explore various perspectives on current events, and the skill of comparing and contrasting to analyze characters in a Shakespearean play.

3. **Metaintelligence—intelligence investigating itself** *(teaching* about *multiple intelligences).* Lessons that deal with metaintelligence processes are concerned with teaching students about their own multiple intelligences—how to access them, how to strengthen them, and how to actively use them in learning and in everyday life.

OK, I buy the eight ways of knowing! What does it take to teach in this way? What's involved in lessons that take into account the reality of multiple intelligences in the classroom?

Generally speaking, there are four stages necessary to teach *with* multiple intelligences: awaken, amplify, teach, and transfer (see fig. 0.3).

What Does it Take To Teach Intelligence?

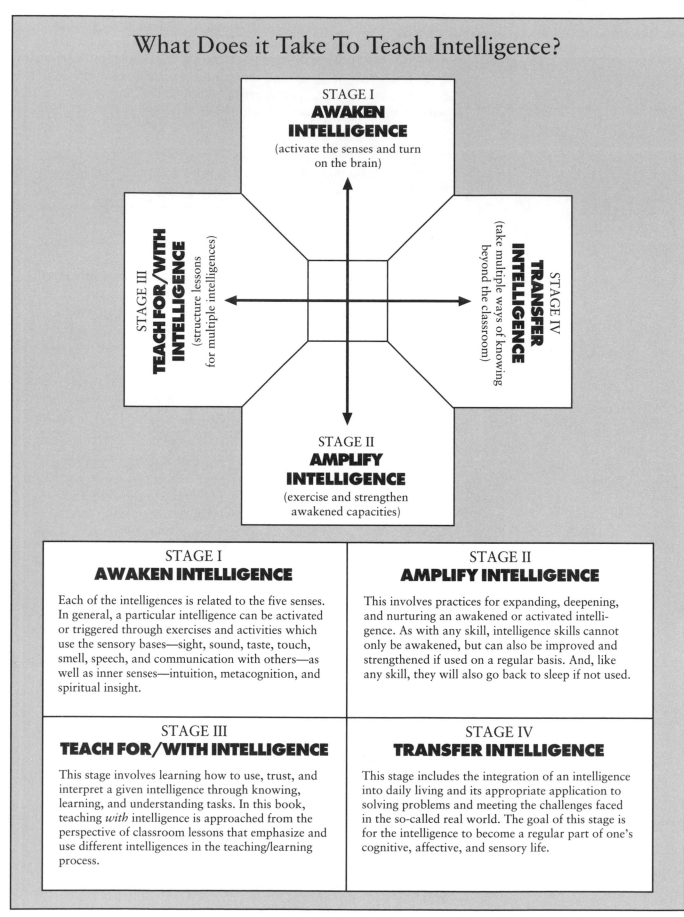

STAGE I
AWAKEN INTELLIGENCE

Each of the intelligences is related to the five senses. In general, a particular intelligence can be activated or triggered through exercises and activities which use the sensory bases—sight, sound, taste, touch, smell, speech, and communication with others—as well as inner senses—intuition, metacognition, and spiritual insight.

STAGE II
AMPLIFY INTELLIGENCE

This involves practices for expanding, deepening, and nurturing an awakened or activated intelligence. As with any skill, intelligence skills cannot only be awakened, but can also be improved and strengthened if used on a regular basis. And, like any skill, they will also go back to sleep if not used.

STAGE III
TEACH FOR/WITH INTELLIGENCE

This stage involves learning how to use, trust, and interpret a given intelligence through knowing, learning, and understanding tasks. In this book, teaching *with* intelligence is approached from the perspective of classroom lessons that emphasize and use different intelligences in the teaching/learning process.

STAGE IV
TRANSFER INTELLIGENCE

This stage includes the integration of an intelligence into daily living and its appropriate application to solving problems and meeting the challenges faced in the so-called real world. The goal of this stage is for the intelligence to become a regular part of one's cognitive, affective, and sensory life.

Figure 0.3

Stage I: Awaken. We must be aware that we possess multiple ways of knowing and learning and that we must learn various techniques and methodologies for triggering an intelligence within the brain-mind-body system.

Stage II: Amplify. We must learn how particular intelligences (ways of knowing) work; that is, what the various capacities and/or skills are, how to access them, and how to use and understand different intelligence modalities. This involves both practice in strengthening intelligence capacities as well as learning how to interpret and work with the different kinds of information we receive from each intelligence. We must learn to understand the unique language of each intelligence; that is, how each expresses itself. For example, the language of bodily/kinesthetic intelligence is physical movement, *not* words, sentences, writing, and speech.

Stage III: Teach. We must learn how to teach content-based lessons that apply different ways of knowing to the specific content of a given lesson. My first presupposition is that **we can teach *all* students to be more intelligent** in more ways, and on more levels than they (or we) ever dreamed. My second presupposition is that ***anything* can be taught and learned through all of the intelligences.** This means that we as teachers must learn how to use the intelligences in the teaching and learning process. About ninety-five percent of the material we have to teach comes prepackaged in a verbal/linguistic or logical/mathematical form. However, in planning lessons that teach this material, we need not be bound by this packaging. My goal in writing this book is to help you learn to design and implement lessons that emphasize all intelligences.

Stage IV: Transfer. We must teach our students how to use all of the intelligences to improve their effectiveness in dealing with the issues, challenges, and problems we face in the task of daily living. This is primarily a matter of approaching these matters on multiple levels, with a variety of problem-solving methods that use different intelligences.

The model in figure 0.3 is one I used as the basic structure for the chapters in *Eight Ways of Knowing*. In this book, I use it to demonstrate the fundamental dynamics that I believe need to be present in lessons that are designed to emphasize the different ways of knowing and learning when teaching content-based information.

Let's get practical now. Enough theory! How do I plan lessons that take into account multiple intelligences? What is the nitty-gritty of this?

I am glad you asked, for this is what the rest of the book is about! Each of the following chapters presents a model lesson that emphasizes one of the intelligences as the primary mode of knowing and learning. As a preface to these lessons I must mention that in the normal person the intelligences operate in concert with each other, generally in well orchestrated ways, although certain of the intelligences do tend to be stronger or more developed than others. Therefore in each of the lessons you will notice all of the intelligences get into the act, so to speak, even though the lessons are designed to focus on and use one intelligence in particular. In my own teaching I generally try to involve at least three ways of knowing *beyond* the verbal/linguistic and logical/mathematical. I believe this is a good rule of thumb for classroom lessons as well. Remember, the more intelligences you can incorporate into a lesson the deeper and more thorough the learning will be.

The Multiple Intelligences Toolbox (fig. 0.4) contains practical techniques, methods, tools, and media for accessing the eight intelligences. They must be used in conjunction with other parts of the lesson and adapted for dealing with content-based information, but these tools can help you move quickly into various ways of knowing in a lesson. In each lesson I have selected several tools from the toolbox and integrated them into the lesson. The tools selected for a given lesson are checkmarked on the lesson palettes. (See Appendix A, pp. 142–145 for a more detailed description of the tools.)

The elements of the remaining chapters of this book are as follows:

1. **Lesson Palette.** The use of the palette as a metaphor for lesson planning is a technique I have found very helpful to remind myself that, as teachers, we are artists who are creating curriculum eventfulness for students. The palette can help you select tools that are appropriate for your objectives as well as help you see how to integrate the different intelligence tools into the lesson. The palette for each lesson lists the ten tools (from the toolbox) for the intelligence being emphasized. On each palette I have checkmarked the specific tools used in the lesson as well as the other intelligences that are involved. (See Appendix A, p. 146 for a blank palette you can use on your own).

2. **The Lesson at a Glance.** This two-page model is a brief overview of the processes of *awakening, amplifying, teaching,* and *transferring* as they apply to the intelligence being emphasized in the lesson. (See Appendix A, p. 147 for a blank lesson plan staging model you can use on your own.)

3. **Lesson Procedures.** The lessons are intended to be models from which you can design your own lessons. They are step-by-step procedures written from the perspective of the teacher—what you do to get students involved in using their multiple intelligences in the classroom. In the left margin is the metacognitive processing of the lesson and is, in my opinion, the most important part of the book. The discussion explains what is going on in the lesson from the perspective of the research on multiple intelligences and also refers to brain functions associated with the intelligences (see fig. 0.5).

SkyLight Training and Publishing Inc.

Logical/Mathematical

- Abstract Symbols/ Formulas
- Calculation
- Deciphering Codes
- Forcing Relationships
- Graphic/Cognitive Organizers
- Logic/Pattern Games
- Number Sequences/ Patterns
- Outlining
- Problem Solving
- Syllogisms

Verbal/Linguistic

- Creative Writing
- Formal Speaking
- Humor/Jokes
- Impromptu Speaking
- Journal/Diary Keeping
- Poetry
- Reading
- Storytelling/Story Creation
- Verbal Debate
- Vocabulary

Visual/Spatial

- Active Imagination
- Color/Texture Schemes
- Drawing
- Guided Imagery/ Visualizing
- Mind Mapping
- Montage/Collage
- Painting
- Patterns/Designs
- Pretending/Fantasy
- Sculpting

Musical/Rhythmic

- Environmental Sounds
- Instrumental Sounds
- Music Composition/Creation
- Music Performance
- Percussion Vibrations
- Rapping
- Rhythmic Patterns
- Singing/Humming
- Tonal Patterns
- Vocal Sounds/Tones

Bodily/Kinesthetic

- Body Language/Physical Gestures
- Body Sculpture/Tableaus
- Dramatic Enactment
- Folk/Creative Dance
- Gymnastic Routines
- Human Graph
- Inventing
- Physical Exercise/Martial Arts
- Role Playing/Mime
- Sports Games

Interpersonal

- Collaborative Skills Teaching
- Cooperative Learning Strategies
- Empathy Practices
- Giving Feedback
- Group Projects
- Intuiting Others' Feelings
- Jigsaw
- Person-to-Person Communication
- Receiving Feedback
- Sensing Others' Motives

Intrapersonal

- Altered States of Consciousness Practices
- Emotional Processing
- Focusing/Concentration Skills
- Higher-Order Reasoning
- Independent Studies/Projects
- Know Thyself Procedures
- Metacognition Techniques
- Mindfulness Practices
- Silent Reflection Methods
- Thinking Strategies

Naturalist

- Archetypal Pattern Recognition
- Caring for Plants/Animals
- Conservation Practices
- Environment Feedback
- Hands-On Labs
- Nature Encounters/Field Trips
- Nature Observation
- Natural World Simulations
- Species Classification (organic/inorganic)
- Sensory Stimulation Exercises

(Note: For a detailed explanation of the tools, see Appendix A, pp. 142–145.)

Figure 0.4

Views of the Brain

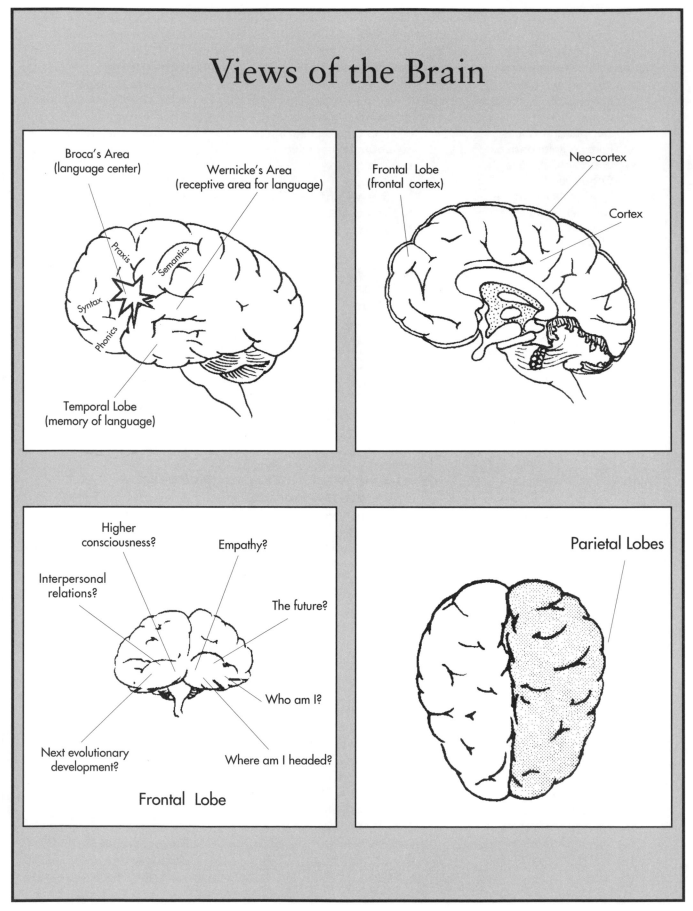

Figure 0.5

SkyLight Training and Publishing Inc.

4. **Spiral Adaptations of the Lesson.** Each lesson focuses on one grade level (elementary, middle, or secondary). I have therefore included this section in order to provide some suggestions for other levels. This adaptation relies on the research of Jerome Brunner on spiraling the curriculum. He said that we can teach anything to anyone, at any age, if we as teachers take the time to get inside their worldview and speak the language that is meaningful to them in that world and at that age.

5. **Assessment Tips.** These assessment ideas are related to the completed lesson. These ideas will make extensive use of student portfolios (see fig. 0.6) and journals (see Appendix A, pp. 148–151 for models).

6. **Look to the Past** and **Look to the Future.** These lesson palettes are designed to help the teacher reflect on how a past or future lesson could be restructured to incorporate the intelligence being emphasized in the lesson.

7. **Lesson Planning Ideas.** This is a chart of ideas for lessons in a given intelligence area. I have tried to address all major subject areas we teach in our schools, such as history, mathematics, language arts, social studies, science, health, geography, computer science, physical education, industrial arts, home economics, and fine arts. The ideas in the chart are lesson seedlings which you may want to plant, water, put in the sunlight, and see if they grow. Incidentally, I would love to hear about any that do grow!

I hope you have fun with this book and that it sparks many new ideas for you and your students. I believe that the next stages of the research on multiple intelligences will happen in the laboratory of the normal school classroom. It will be based on what you discover as you conduct various experiments with eight ways of teaching, helping kids activate and use their eight ways of knowing.

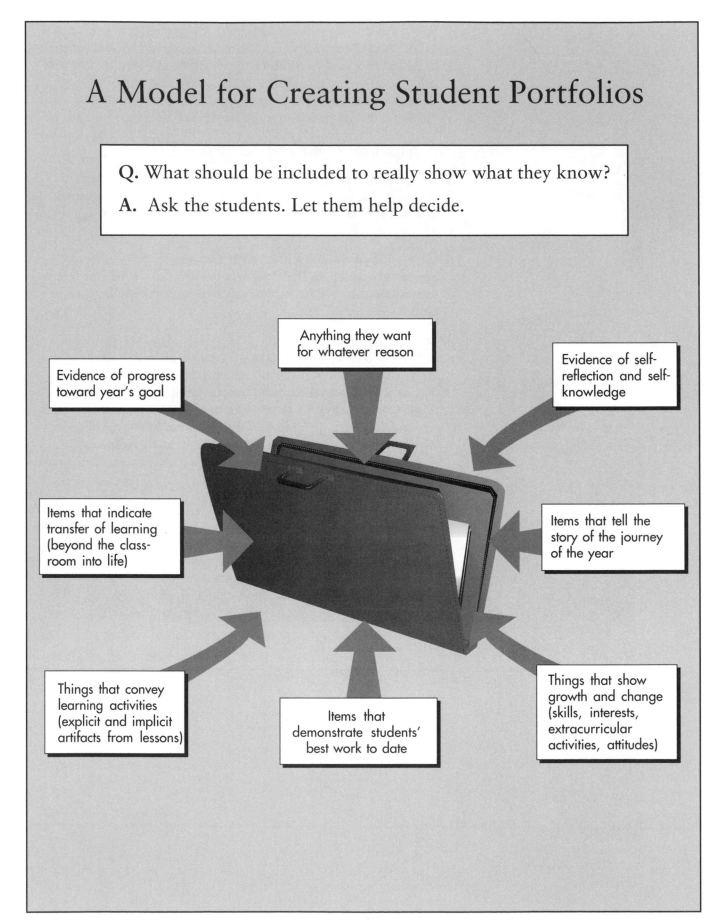

A Model for Creating Student Portfolios

Q. What should be included to really show what they know?

A. Ask the students. Let them help decide.

Anything they want for whatever reason

Evidence of progress toward year's goal

Evidence of self-reflection and self-knowledge

Items that indicate transfer of learning (beyond the classroom into life)

Items that tell the story of the journey of the year

Things that convey learning activities (explicit and implicit artifacts from lessons)

Items that demonstrate students' best work to date

Things that show growth and change (skills, interests, extracurricular activities, attitudes)

Figure 0.6

TEACHING WITH
VERBAL/LINGUISTIC
INTELLIGENCE

EXPLORING NATURAL
OBJECTS

A General Science Lesson:
Elementary School Level

Lesson Palette: *Verbal/Linguistic* Emphasis

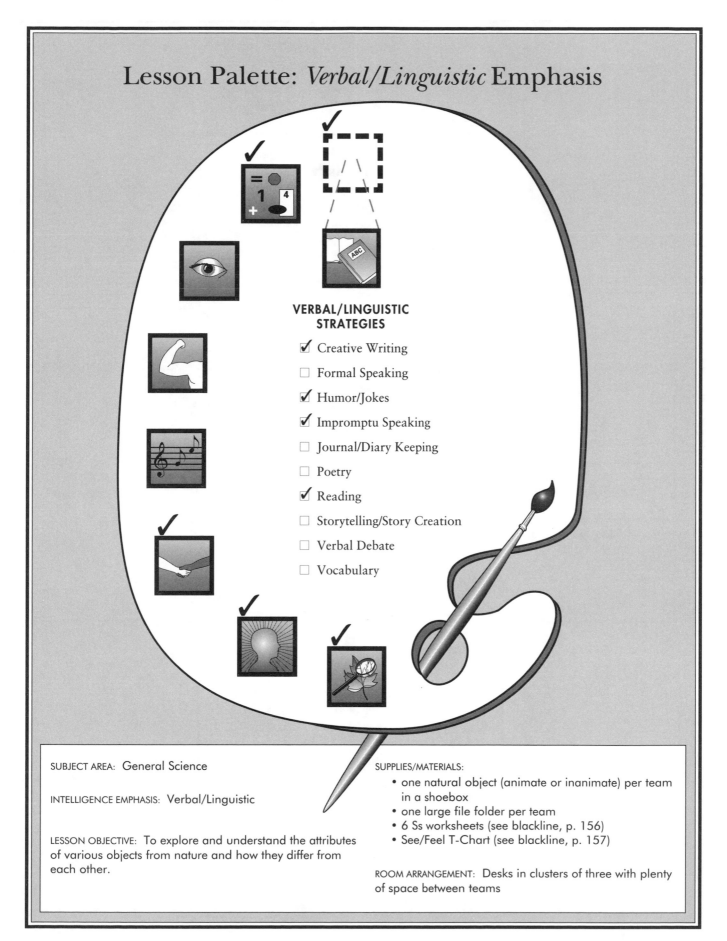

VERBAL/LINGUISTIC STRATEGIES

- ☑ Creative Writing
- ☐ Formal Speaking
- ☑ Humor/Jokes
- ☑ Impromptu Speaking
- ☐ Journal/Diary Keeping
- ☐ Poetry
- ☑ Reading
- ☐ Storytelling/Story Creation
- ☐ Verbal Debate
- ☐ Vocabulary

SUBJECT AREA: General Science

INTELLIGENCE EMPHASIS: Verbal/Linguistic

LESSON OBJECTIVE: To explore and understand the attributes of various objects from nature and how they differ from each other.

SUPPLIES/MATERIALS:
- one natural object (animate or inanimate) per team in a shoebox
- one large file folder per team
- 6 Ss worksheets (see blackline, p. 156)
- See/Feel T-Chart (see blackline, p. 157)

ROOM ARRANGEMENT: Desks in clusters of three with plenty of space between teams

THE LESSON . . .

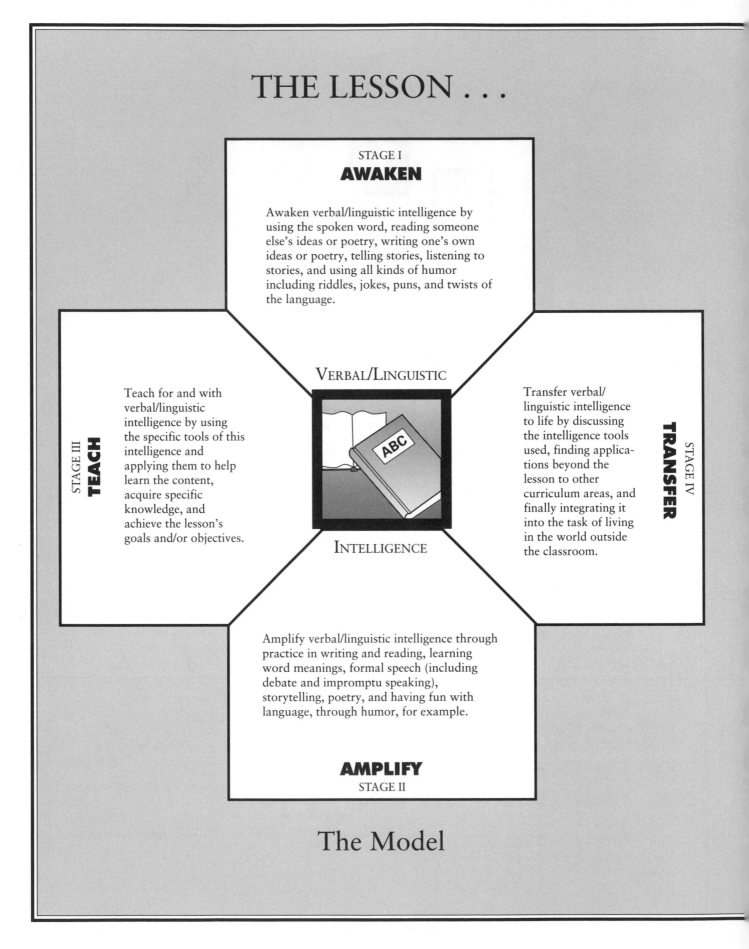

STAGE I

AWAKEN

Awaken verbal/linguistic intelligence by using the spoken word, reading someone else's ideas or poetry, writing one's own ideas or poetry, telling stories, listening to stories, and using all kinds of humor including riddles, jokes, puns, and twists of the language.

VERBAL/LINGUISTIC

STAGE III
TEACH

Teach for and with verbal/linguistic intelligence by using the specific tools of this intelligence and applying them to help learn the content, acquire specific knowledge, and achieve the lesson's goals and/or objectives.

STAGE IV
TRANSFER

Transfer verbal/ linguistic intelligence to life by discussing the intelligence tools used, finding applications beyond the lesson to other curriculum areas, and finally integrating it into the task of living in the world outside the classroom.

INTELLIGENCE

Amplify verbal/linguistic intelligence through practice in writing and reading, learning word meanings, formal speech (including debate and impromptu speaking), storytelling, poetry, and having fun with language, through humor, for example.

AMPLIFY
STAGE II

The Model

...AT A GLANCE

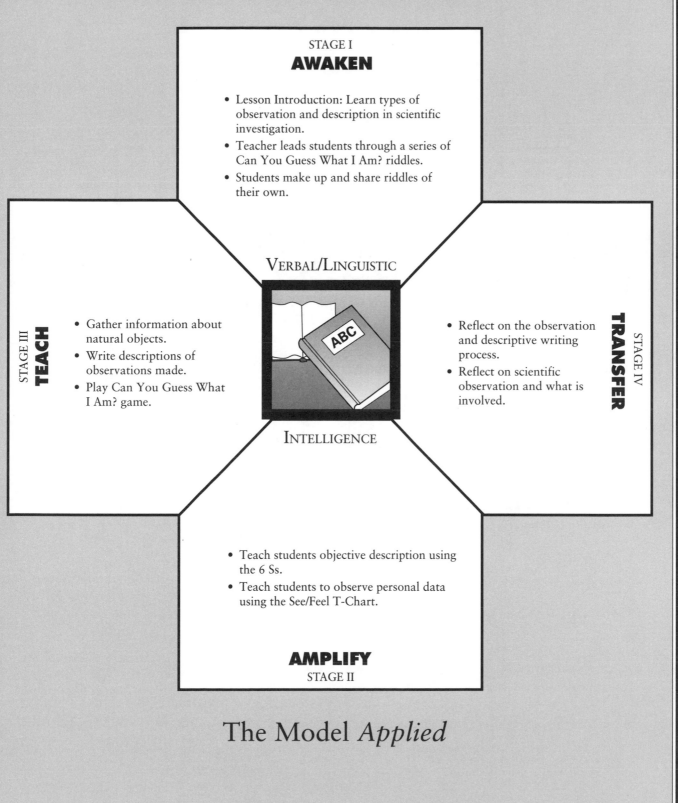

STAGE I

AWAKEN

- Lesson Introduction: Learn types of observation and description in scientific investigation.
- Teacher leads students through a series of Can You Guess What I Am? riddles.
- Students make up and share riddles of their own.

VERBAL/LINGUISTIC

STAGE III

TEACH

- Gather information about natural objects.
- Write descriptions of observations made.
- Play Can You Guess What I Am? game.

STAGE IV

TRANSFER

- Reflect on the observation and descriptive writing process.
- Reflect on scientific observation and what is involved.

INTELLIGENCE

- Teach students objective description using the 6 Ss.
- Teach students to observe personal data using the See/Feel T-Chart.

AMPLIFY

STAGE II

The Model *Applied*

Exploring Objects

A Science Lesson with

Verbal/Linguistic Intelligence

Lesson Procedures

INTRODUCTION

The world is full of interesting and surprising things that can be discovered if we learn to pay attention. In this science lesson students will observe natural objects with their senses (objective observation) and their own feelings or responses about what they are observing (subjective observation). They will then use this information to play the game, Can You Guess What I Am? Tell the students that the lesson will emphasize verbal/linguistic intelligence, so they should pay attention to this during the lesson.

Although the main emphasis of this lesson is teaching with verbal/linguistic intelligence, four other intelligences are consciously employed as well: interpersonal intelligence through cooperative group interactions, logical/mathematical intelligence through the use of cognitive organizers, interpersonal intelligence through individual writing (especially about feelings), and naturalist intelligence through observing a natural object through the senses.

☛ Verbal/linguistic intelligence is primarily located in the area of the left hemisphere of the brain known as Broca's Area (see fig. 0.5, p. 12). The particular mental functions that are active when verbal/linguistic intelligence has been turned on involve an acute sensitivity to the sound, rhythm, inflection, and meter of words; a sensitivity to the order among words and the various meanings and shades of meaning of words; and an interest in the different practical uses of language. Please refer to the Multiple Intelligences Capacities Wheel (fig. 0.2, p. 6) to see capacities that are active when working with verbal/linguistic intelligence.

STAGE I

☛ Here riddles are used as the trigger. When the brain is presented with a riddle, verbal/linguistic intelligence immediately kicks into gear to try to figure it out. It begins searching for clues within the linguistic structure of the riddle and tries to make connections between the riddle and

AWAKEN

1. Begin with a series of riddles. Have students see if they can guess the answers:

   • Of all the things in the world, I am the shortest and the longest, the fastest and the slowest. I am the thing people waste the most. Yet they need me more than anything else. What am I? *(Answer: time)*

prior knowledge. It starts looking for word associations. When students are asked to think of their own riddles to stump the class, the language center of the brain is stimulated even more, for you are asking them to be creative and have fun with their language.

Both the groans and the laughter, as well as the *Of course, why didn't I figure that out?* at the end of a riddle, are indications that verbal/linguistic intelligence has been awakened and that it is now ready for action.

- Everyone needs my help. I dig out tiny caves and put gold and silver in them. I also build bridges of silver and make crowns of gold. Sooner or later everyone needs my help. Yet many people are afraid to let me help them. Who am I? *(Answer: a dentist)*

- I have eyes but I see nothing. I have ears but hear nothing. I have a mouth but I cannot speak. I always will look the way I look now. If I am young I will stay young. If I am old I will stay old. What am I? *(Answer: a person in a painting or photograph)*

2. Ask students if they know any riddles they think could stump the class.

STAGE II

☞ Practice using the awakened intelligence will improve it. In addition to the intelligence itself getting stronger, we become more familiar with it, and understand more about how it works. We learn how to interpret information we get from it, how to use it most effectively, and in what situations it can most enhance our learning.

Teaching about the 6 Ss introduces the students to a specific intellectual tool you want them to use later in the content part of the lesson itself. It is crucial that you both give them guidelines for using the tool and demonstrate how to use it. Your demonstration should be as close as possible to what you are going to ask them to do with the content of the lesson. Cognitive research has shown that any thinking skill we want our students to have must be explicitly taught and, furthermore, students must have an opportunity to practice it. I believe that the same is true of all of the intellectual capacities. We were born with them, but we must be taught how to use them and then be given opportunities to practice if we are to become masters of our intellectual capacities. Working with the 6 Ss also accesses logical/mathematical intelligence as students learn new patterns for thinking.

 **AMPLIFY**

1. Pass out the 6 Ss worksheet to the students (see blackline, p. 156). Explain that in order for students to describe something they must learn to recognize its attributes. The 6 Ss worksheet can help students with this job. Explain the worksheet as follows:

6 Ss = Sight — the color, image, or look of something
        Sound — the noise, tone, and voice of something
        Smell — the odor, aroma, and scent of something
        Sense (tactile) — the taste or touch of something
        Size — the height, weight, width, and depth of something
        Speciality — the use of something or what it's good for

Explain that the 6 Ss worksheet allows students to use their senses to determine what an object is and how it differs from another object. Scientists also use the 6 Ss when they are studying something.

2. Now practice using the 6 Ss as a class. Draw the 6 Ss chart on the board or overhead. Choose an object in the classroom that all students can see and write the name of the object at the top of the chart.

3. Have students number off by sixes to form six groups. Assign each group one of the 6 Ss. Now ask students to give you attributes that describe the object according to their assigned part of the 6 Ss.

4. Reflect with the class for a few minutes:
   - How did the 6 Ss help?
   - Which S was most difficult? easiest?
   - What questions do you have about using the 6 Ss?

STAGE III

☞ By placing students in cooperative groups you bring in interpersonal intelligence skills as well.

☞ The very fact that you are using objects from nature will stimulate the naturalist intelligence.

☞ Students use the intellectual skill you teach in this part of the lesson to gain information and explore the meaning of the lesson content. The key assumption of the previous two parts of the lesson is that the more aware students become of their own intelligence and how it works, the more they will know how to use that intelligence to access the necessary information and knowledge from a lesson. Now they have a chance to do just that. Writing the sentences helps them pull together the team's brainstorm for themselves and to enhance their own understanding.

☞ The See/Feel T-Chart again draws on logical/mathematical intelligence. You teach a thinking skill and then provide students with a chance to practice and use it on their own.

☞ After brainstorming information on the worksheet with their cooperative group, students are asked to translate their observations and feelings into writing. The creative writing exercise allows students to assimilate the team's brainstorm into sentences that are meaningful to them as

 **TEACH**

1. Group students in teams of three and assign a role to each student: lab assistant (gathers materials for the team), organizer (keeps team on task and makes sure all parts of the assignment are completed), and encourager (gives group support and keeps them motivated).

2. Have the lab assistants come to the lab table and get a box for their team. In each box you have placed an object from nature such as an interesting rock, a large pine cone, a twisted, gnarly twig, a flower, a lump of earth, etc. Tell students not to let other teams see their objects. They should sit so the other team cannot see the objects and use their file folders as screens to hide the objects.

3. **Activity 1.** Lead students through the following steps:

   a. Have each student write the name of the object on their 6 Ss worksheet.

   b. Prompt teams to use the 6 Ss to describe the object that is in their box.

   c. Instruct each individual to write three sentences in the space provided on the 6 Ss worksheet that tell things about the object the team has been analyzing.

   d. Tell each student quietly read their sentences to the rest of the team so the team can check for the writer's understanding.

4. Now pass out the See/Feel T-Chart (see blackline, p. 157) to the teams. Choose an object in the classroom that all students can see, and model for them how to use the See/Feel T-Chart:

   a. As you look at the object, find shapes, designs, and patterns that are interesting to you. Write these on the t-chart under What I See.

   b. Also try to find the shapes of animals, human faces, etc. in the design of the object and point these out to the students. Write them on the t-chart.

   c. Now spend a couple of minutes thinking out loud for the class, describing your own feelings about the object you have been describing. Record these feelings on the t-chart under How I Feel.

5. **Activity 2.** Lead students through the following steps:

   a. Instruct the students to write the name of their objects on the second worksheet.

   b. Tell them to do what you just did but with their own object—look for interesting shapes, patterns, designs, and pictures in their object. Ask them to record these things in the column labeled What I See.

SkyLight Training and Publishing Inc.

individuals. Here you are likewise accessing intrapersonal intelligence as students look within at their own feelings and responses.

(Note: Encourage maximum creativity in looking at and describing the object. Remember there are no right answers! Whatever they see and/or find in their object is there for them.)

c. Have the teams talk quietly about how they feel about the object (e.g., interested, bored, excited, etc.).

d. In the space provided on the worksheet, have each individual write two sentences: one about what the team saw or found in the object and one sentence about how they feel about it.

e. Have each student quietly read their sentences to the rest of the team so the team can check for the writer's understanding.

6. Have the lab assistant put the objects back in the box and return them to the lab table.

7. Tell the class that they are now going to play a game called Can You Guess What I Am? that will let them practice describing things to others.

☛ The Can You Guess What I Am? game further engages verbal/linguistic skills by asking students to speak extemporaneously about their object in response to questions from others. This requires a synthesis and deeper understanding of their earlier work of describing the objects.

a. Have students form new groups. Tell them to keep the identity of their original group's object a secret because their new group is going to try to guess what the object is.

b. The new group will try to guess the object by asking questions that can be answered yes or no.

c. When the group thinks they know the mystery object they may guess. Then move on to another person until all have had a turn.

TRANSFER

STAGE IV

☛ The goal of the transfer section of the lesson is to help students make the lesson relevant to their lives outside the classroom. Here we want to go beyond the lesson itself, into other curriculum areas, and finally beyond the formal classroom setting.

Students discuss the two observation exercises with the 6 Ss and the See/Feel T-Chart, their reactions to them and other situations where they could be used. Then in finishing the sentences, they have an opportunity to make conscious the learnings that happened in the lesson. This also helps them distill the essential parts of the lesson for themselves.

1. Start at the beginning of the lesson asking some or all of the following questions of the whole class:

• What part was easy in this lesson? What was hard? What was fun?

• What did you like about the 6 Ss? About the See/Feel T-Chart?

• What did you not like about these charts?

• When could we use the 6 Ss and the See/Feel T-Chart in other subjects?

2. Now spend a few minutes having students talk in their game groups about what they learned in the lesson. Have each person in the game group write and then read their answers to the following sentences:

One new thing I learned about natural objects is_____.

One new thing I learned about working on a team is_____.

SPIRAL ADAPTATIONS OF THE LESSON

Middle School Level

1. Focus the lesson on learning the scientific method for accurate observation and the ability to accurately record observations.

2. Teach about and have students practice two thinking patterns involved in scientific experiments:

    - looking at and analyzing an object (objective)
    - looking at yourself and your response to the object being observed (subjective)

3. Have students write detailed descriptive paragraphs that report on their factual observations about the objects, and their personal responses and reactions to the object.

Secondary School Level

1. Focus the lesson on three thinking/observation patterns at work in science: empirical observation (the facts, the senses), subjective responses (feelings, emotions, etc. about what is being observed), and creative interpretation (trying to fit observations into existing paradigms).

2. Practice each type of thinking/observation in conducting science lab experiments. For each type, have students keep an Experiment Log in which they record what they have learned using each of the three methods of observation. Ask them to report on what they have observed to other students.

3. Have students write the steps for a scientific observation project that uses all three types of observation.

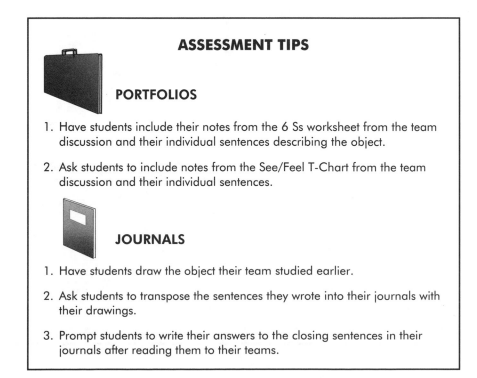

ASSESSMENT TIPS

PORTFOLIOS

1. Have students include their notes from the 6 Ss worksheet from the team discussion and their individual sentences describing the object.

2. Ask students to include notes from the See/Feel T-Chart from the team discussion and their individual sentences.

JOURNALS

1. Have students draw the object their team studied earlier.

2. Ask students to transpose the sentences they wrote into their journals with their drawings.

3. Prompt students to write their answers to the closing sentences in their journals after reading them to their teams.

Look to the Past . . .

Rethink a lesson you have completed recently. How would you restructure it to teach *for* and *with* verbal/linguistic intelligence?

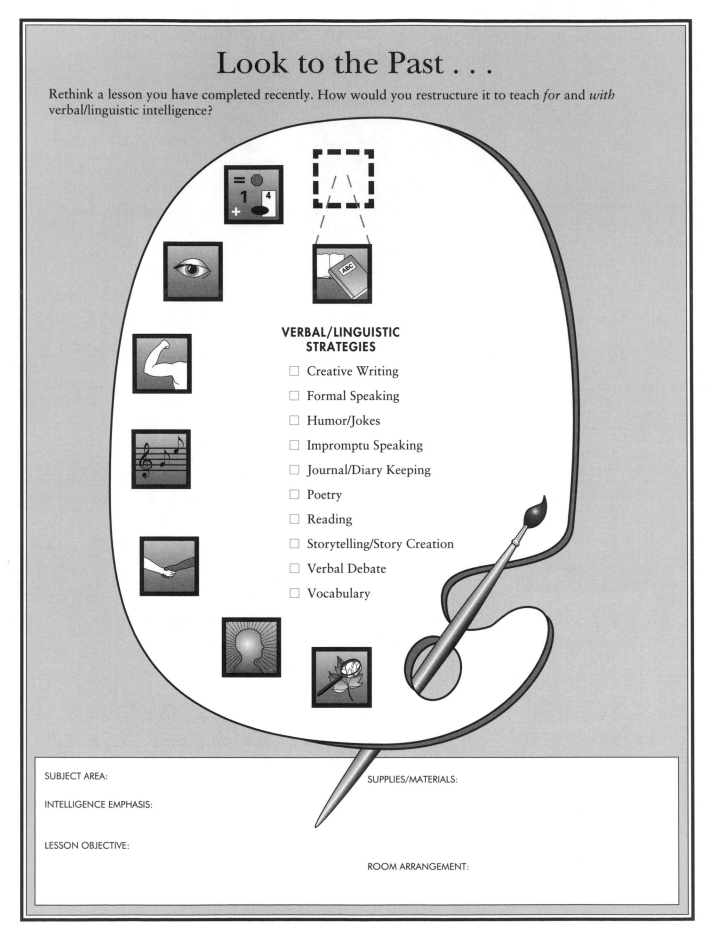

VERBAL/LINGUISTIC STRATEGIES

☐ Creative Writing

☐ Formal Speaking

☐ Humor/Jokes

☐ Impromptu Speaking

☐ Journal/Diary Keeping

☐ Poetry

☐ Reading

☐ Storytelling/Story Creation

☐ Verbal Debate

☐ Vocabulary

SUBJECT AREA:

INTELLIGENCE EMPHASIS:

LESSON OBJECTIVE:

SUPPLIES/MATERIALS:

ROOM ARRANGEMENT:

SkyLight Training and Publishing Inc.

Look to the Future . . .

Think about a lesson you have coming up in the near future. How would you structure it to teach *for* and *with* verbal/linguistic intelligence?

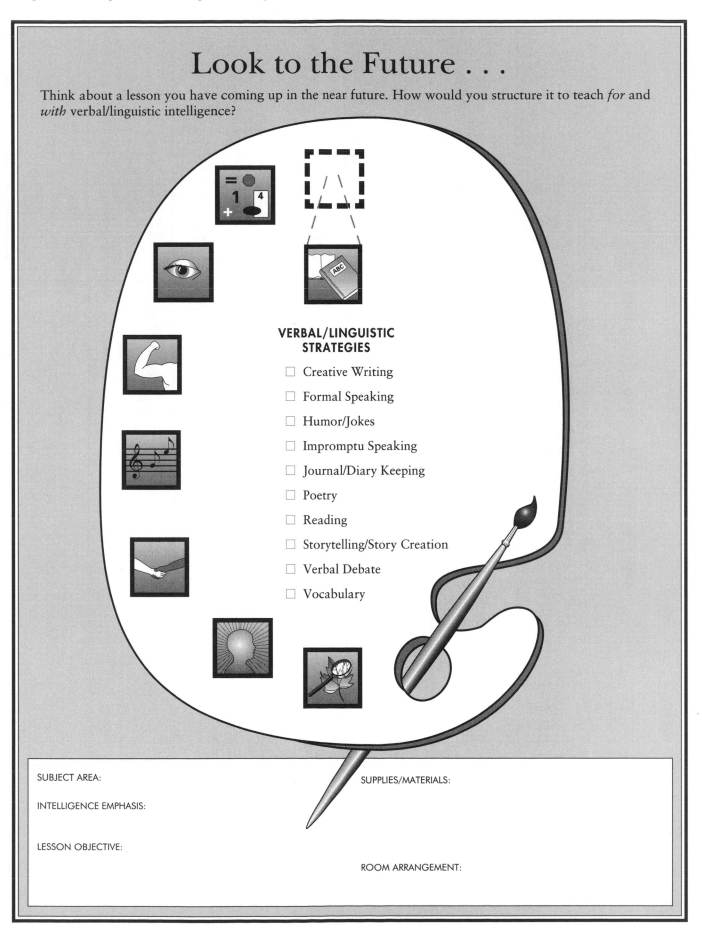

VERBAL/LINGUISTIC STRATEGIES

- ☐ Creative Writing
- ☐ Formal Speaking
- ☐ Humor/Jokes
- ☐ Impromptu Speaking
- ☐ Journal/Diary Keeping
- ☐ Poetry
- ☐ Reading
- ☐ Storytelling/Story Creation
- ☐ Verbal Debate
- ☐ Vocabulary

SUBJECT AREA:

INTELLIGENCE EMPHASIS:

LESSON OBJECTIVE:

SUPPLIES/MATERIALS:

ROOM ARRANGEMENT:

SkyLight Training and Publishing Inc.

Lesson Planning Ideas
Verbal/Linguistic

HISTORY	MATHEMATICS	LANGUAGE ARTS	SCIENCE & HEALTH	GLOBAL STUDIES & GEOGRAPHY	FAMILY/CONSUMER SCIENCES, INDUSTRIAL TECHNOLOGY, & PE	FINE ARTS
Play What's My Line? with figures from history	Write a series of story problems for others to solve	Teach concept mapping** to help remember content	Write a humorous story using science vocabulary or formulas	Read stories, myths, and poetry from other cultures	Give verbal explanation of gymnastic routines	Listen to a piece of music and make up a story about it
Debate important issues and decisions from the past	Explain how to work a problem to others while they follow	Write a sequel or next episode to a story or play	Create a diary on The Life of a Red Blood Cell	Hold Countries of the World spelling and pronunciation bee	Write instructions for use and care of shop machines	Verbally describe an object while a partner draws it
Create limericks about key historical events	Make up puns using math vocabulary or terms	Create crossword puzzles or word jumbles for vocabulary words	Write steps used in an experiment so someone else can do it	Keep an Insights From Other Cultures for Us log	Tell another how to run a word processing program—then do it	Tell a partner the steps to a dance while they perform it
Study poetry from different periods of history	Solve problems with a partner—one solves and one explains process	Play New Word for the Day* game	Make up an imaginary conversation between parts of the body	Study a road map and give verbal instructions to get someplace	Pretend you are a radio sportscaster describing a game in process	Turn a Greek or Shakespearean tragedy into a situation comedy
Compile a notebook of history jokes	Create poems telling when to use different math operations	Practice impromptu speaking and writing	Give a speech on Ten Steps to Healthful Living	Learn basic conversation in several foreign languages	Play Recipe Jeopardy—make questions for answers given	Describe an emotion or mood and play music it suggests

* See Glossary
** See Glossary and Appendix C

SkyLight Training and Publishing Inc.

TEACHING WITH
LOGICAL/MATHEMATICAL
INTELLIGENCE

UNDERSTANDING OTHER
CULTURES

A Social Studies Lesson:
Middle School Level

Lesson Palette: *Logical/Mathematical* Emphasis

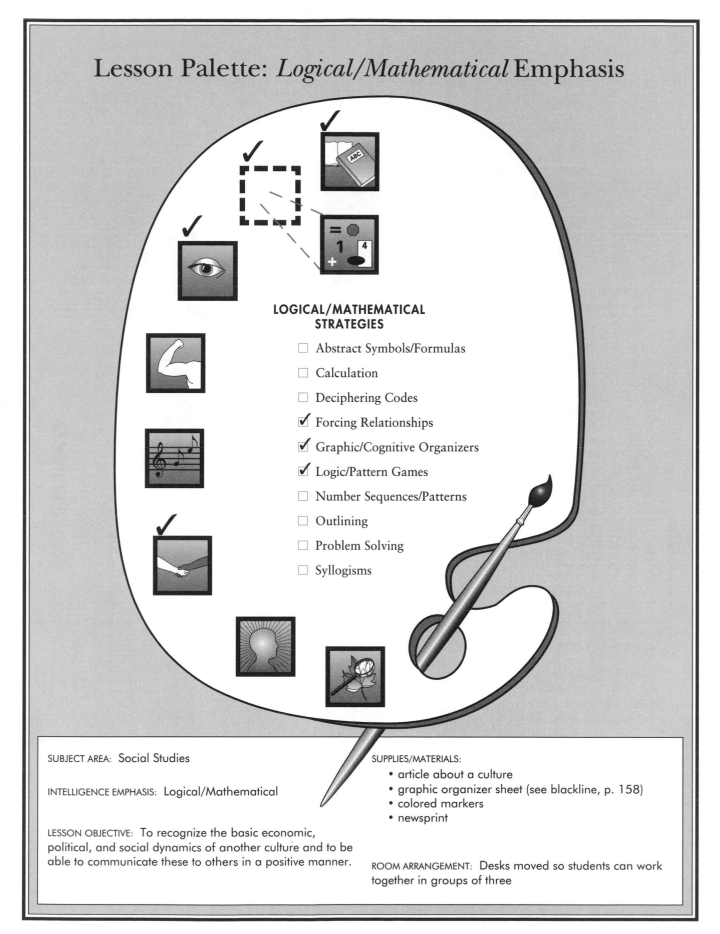

LOGICAL/MATHEMATICAL STRATEGIES

- ☐ Abstract Symbols/Formulas
- ☐ Calculation
- ☐ Deciphering Codes
- ☑ Forcing Relationships
- ☑ Graphic/Cognitive Organizers
- ☑ Logic/Pattern Games
- ☐ Number Sequences/Patterns
- ☐ Outlining
- ☐ Problem Solving
- ☐ Syllogisms

SUBJECT AREA: Social Studies

INTELLIGENCE EMPHASIS: Logical/Mathematical

LESSON OBJECTIVE: To recognize the basic economic, political, and social dynamics of another culture and to be able to communicate these to others in a positive manner.

SUPPLIES/MATERIALS:
- article about a culture
- graphic organizer sheet (see blackline, p. 158)
- colored markers
- newsprint

ROOM ARRANGEMENT: Desks moved so students can work together in groups of three

THE LESSON . . .

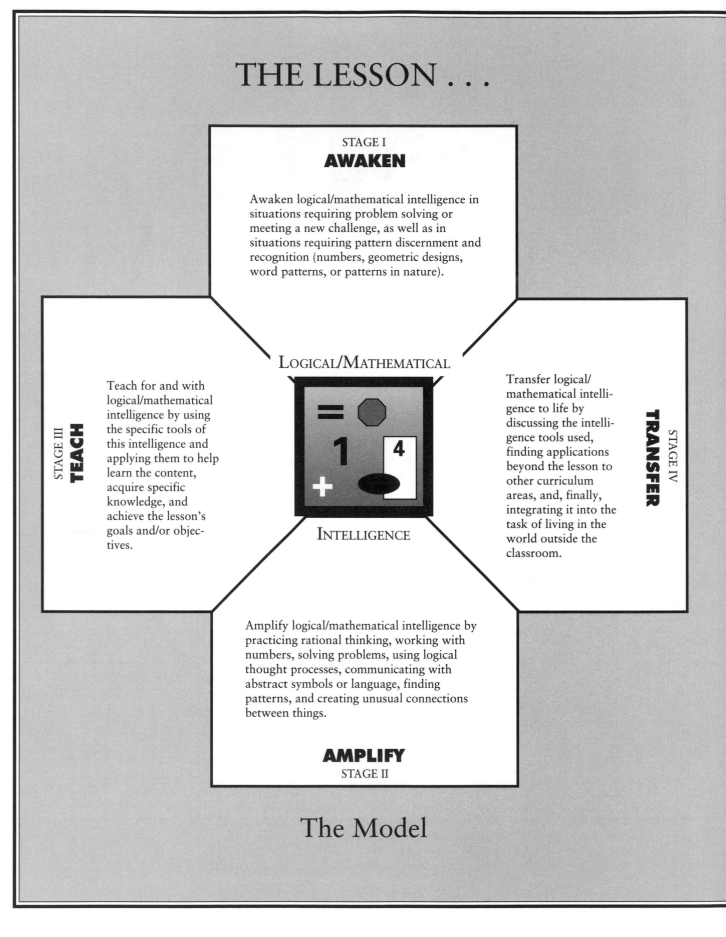

STAGE I
AWAKEN

Awaken logical/mathematical intelligence in situations requiring problem solving or meeting a new challenge, as well as in situations requiring pattern discernment and recognition (numbers, geometric designs, word patterns, or patterns in nature).

LOGICAL/MATHEMATICAL

STAGE III
TEACH

Teach for and with logical/mathematical intelligence by using the specific tools of this intelligence and applying them to help learn the content, acquire specific knowledge, and achieve the lesson's goals and/or objectives.

STAGE IV
TRANSFER

Transfer logical/ mathematical intelligence to life by discussing the intelligence tools used, finding applications beyond the lesson to other curriculum areas, and, finally, integrating it into the task of living in the world outside the classroom.

INTELLIGENCE

Amplify logical/mathematical intelligence by practicing rational thinking, working with numbers, solving problems, using logical thought processes, communicating with abstract symbols or language, finding patterns, and creating unusual connections between things.

AMPLIFY
STAGE II

The Model

SkyLight Training and Publishing Inc.

...AT A GLANCE

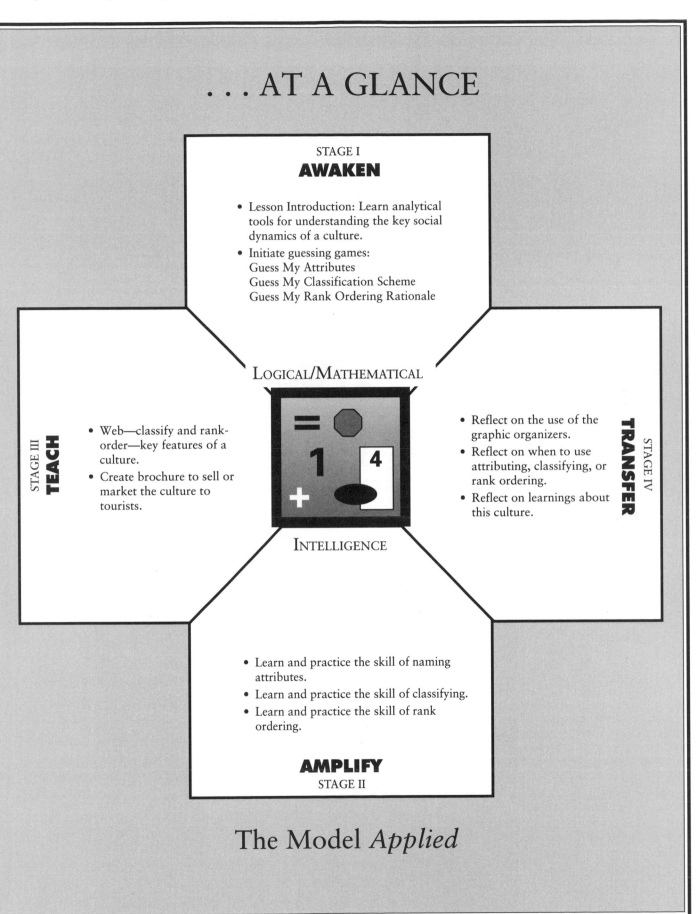

STAGE I
AWAKEN

- Lesson Introduction: Learn analytical tools for understanding the key social dynamics of a culture.
- Initiate guessing games:
  Guess My Attributes
  Guess My Classification Scheme
  Guess My Rank Ordering Rationale

LOGICAL/MATHEMATICAL

STAGE III
TEACH

- Web—classify and rank-order—key features of a culture.
- Create brochure to sell or market the culture to tourists.

INTELLIGENCE

STAGE IV
TRANSFER

- Reflect on the use of the graphic organizers.
- Reflect on when to use attributing, classifying, or rank ordering.
- Reflect on learnings about this culture.

- Learn and practice the skill of naming attributes.
- Learn and practice the skill of classifying.
- Learn and practice the skill of rank ordering.

AMPLIFY
STAGE II

The Model *Applied*

Understanding Other
Cultures

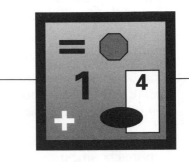

A SOCIAL STUDIES LESSON WITH

Logical/Mathematical Intelligence

Lesson Procedures

INTRODUCTION

☛ Logical/mathematical intelligence represents an intriguing mix of left- and right-brain operations. The ability to read and produce mathematical signs and symbols is a left-brain processing operation not unlike what happens when we learn language. On the other hand, the ability to understand numerical relationships, to discern abstract patterns, and to comprehend logical/mathematical concepts is a right-brain operation. When presented with a problem that needs to be solved or a challenge that must be met, the brain operates like a high-tech computer working to find an answer or solution to the problem or challenge.

The ability to look at another culture or nation and appreciate its gifts and contributions to the world is critical to our global future. In this social studies lesson students will learn how to analyze another culture. First, they will brainstorm different things they know about a culture using a web (see glossary, p. 184 and blackline, p. 178). Second, they will classify their brainstorm list into economic, political, and social dynamics. Third, they will rank order each classified list according to which factors are the most important for the culture. Tell students that the lesson uses logical/ mathematical intelligence and ask them to be aware of using this way of knowing as they work.

The intelligence emphasis of this lesson is logical/mathematical. However, verbal/linguistic intelligence is also used, especially in the initiating guessing games, the writing activities, and creating the television script. Visual/spatial intelligence is employed in the creation of the brochure or flyer for the culture. Interpersonal intelligence is incorporated in and through the cooperative group structure and interaction.

STAGE I

☛ In general, logical/mathematical intelligence is awakened in situations that require problem solving or meeting a new challenge, as well as situations where pattern discernment is needed, such as

AWAKEN

Begin with a series of thinking patterns games:

1. **Can You Guess My Attributes?** Have three students, from different ethnic backgrounds, who have at least three similar attributes

number patterns, geometric designs, and word patterns.

The attributes, classification, and rank order games trigger logical/mathematical intelligence. When the brain is presented with a hidden pattern or rationale, as in these initiating games, its natural love of problem solving automatically engages. It relentlessly tries to find the pattern, the rationale, or the schema to make sense out of the situation. This is the heart of logical/mathematical intelligence.

Once you have told the students that there is a hidden organizing pattern or principle behind what you are doing, watch them struggle, argue, and guess, trying to outfox you in the games. When you see this happening, this is an indication that logical/mathematical intelligence has indeed been awakened and that it is now ready for action.

(e.g., wearing glasses or tennis shoes, curly hair, same height, etc.) come to the front of the room.

Ask the class to guess why you selected this group. Do not be surprised if they find many more common attributes than your original ones!

2. **Can You Guess My Classification Scheme?** Gather a group of ten items from a culture you have been studying. Classify the items into three groups (e.g., by color, shape, texture, size, etc.) and ask students to guess why you put certain items together in the same group.

Again, they will probably come up with more classification categories than you originally had in mind.

3. **Can You Guess My Rank Ordering Rationale?** Show a list of key persons from a culture you have been studying. Rank order the names three different ways (e.g., by dates of death, by best known to least known, etc.). See if students can figure out why you have placed each list in the given order.

STAGE II

☞ Almost anything we do well takes practice. The same is true of working with our intelligence capacities—we must practice using the awakened intelligence and, just like any skill, it will improve. Part of the task here is to train ourselves to understand how the intelligence itself works.

Students need to be introduced to the specific intelligence tools they will be using in the lesson and have an opportunity to practice using them. As you introduce these tools, try to make the practice session activities mirror what you want them to do with the content of the lesson.

The attribute web helps strengthen inductive thinking patterns. By having them talk about their school you have hopefully hooked them with a topic of interest to them. You are likewise accessing verbal/linguistic intelligence through their dialogue about the school and their writing on the web, and interpersonal intelligence by placing them into cooperative groups. In the webbing they brainstorm the basic data on the school.

 **AMPLIFY**

1. Introduce attribute webbing to the students. Explain that the web is a diagram that can help students describe the attributes of something. Ask the class to pretend the school is a culture. Draw a web on the board or overhead and ask students to brainstorm attributes of your school (see blackline, p. 158).

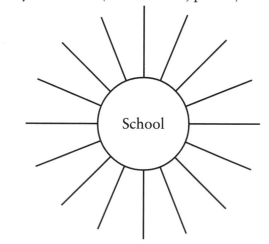

Keep brainstorming until you have at least twenty-five items on the web. Remind students that the key in brainstorming is to accept all ideas. There are no wrong answers as long as they are a response to the brainstorm question.

☛ The classification chart enhances deductive thinking patterns. It asks students to sort their particular brainstorm information from the web into general pre-established categories (in the same way they will do later on with data from another culture) and to make judgments about the data and prioritize it.

3. Introduce classifying to students (see blackline, p. 158). Explain that classifying similar things, or grouping like things together, helps students better understand them. In groups of three, have students briefly classify the brainstorm list of school attributes into four categories—economic, political, social, and symbolic.

CLASSIFICATION CHART

ECONOMIC ATTRIBUTES	POLITICAL ATTRIBUTES	SOCIAL ATTRIBUTES	SYMBOLIC ATTRIBUTES

Have one team share their classification chart. Note similarities and differences with the other teams.

☛ The rank ordering helps students learn and improve their priority thinking skills. To do this they must make judgments about their data and arrive at a consensus. This further activates and uses interpersonal intelligence capacities.

4. Introduce rank ordering to students. Tell students that when they rank order things they will put them in an order according to how important they think each item is. For each category on their classification charts have the teams decide which item is most important for the school and mark that #1, which is second most important and mark that #2, and which is third most important and mark that item #3. Use the ranking ladders (see blackline, p. 158).

RANKING LADDERS

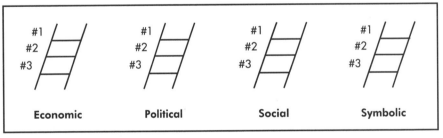

Economic Political Social Symbolic

Have several groups share what they picked as #1 for each category.

5. Tell students that they have been practicing some logical thought processes that are now going to be applied to a social studies lesson. Reflect on the three processes (attribute webbing, classifying, and rank ordering) by asking students these questions:

- Which of the three was easiest? most difficult?
- How did they help your thinking?
- What questions do you have about using these organizers?

SkyLight Training and Publishing Inc.

STAGE III

☞ Students apply the logical/mathematical skills you taught in the amplifying part of the lesson to gain knowledge and explore the meaning of the lesson content.

They begin by studying a section from the textbook which describes a particular culture. Each of the cognitive organizers is then applied in turn to that content, and students are asked to organize and reorganize the basic information into different patterns—attributes that describe a culture, attributes organized under predetermined categories, and attributes ranked in terms of their importance to the culture.

 **TEACH**

1. Using the same groups as before, begin by assigning students the roles of organizer/timekeeper, recorder/materials gatherer, and encourager/motivator within each group. The lesson has two parts: analyzing another culture and using what they have learned to appreciate the culture.

2. **Assignment Part I.** Tell students they will be using the same basic process just used on the school to analyze another culture. Have the students turn to the appropriate page(s) in their textbooks. Put the following instructions on the board or overhead:

Analyzing Another Culture

As a group, complete these tasks:

1. Read the appropriate section(s) of the text.
2. Brainstorm and list the attributes of this culture using the web.
3. Classify the attributes using the economic, political, social, symbolic classification chart.
4. Rank order the first, second, and third most important factor of economic, political, social, and symbolic life for each column on the chart.

---

a. Ask students if they have any questions about the assignment. Have the materials person gather supplies for the group—newsprint, markers, and the graphic organizers worksheet (see blackline, p. 158).

b. When the teams have finished Part I, have them post their graphic organizers somewhere where they can easily see them.

3. **Assignment Part II.** Tell students they are now going to play a game with the analysis they have been doing of this culture. Post the following on the board or overhead:

☞ The final stage of the lesson is a creative thinking process in which students must synthesize what they have learned about the culture and communicate it to others. Two additional intelligences get into the act at this point: verbal/linguistic through the creative writing involved in making up the advertisement and visual/spatial through the creation of the brochure or flyer. Make sure you have plenty of colored markers and/or paints for them to use at this point.

Appreciating Another Culture

As a team, pretend that you are a travel agency that is trying to convince tourists to vacation in this culture. Using the items on your newsprint, your team is to create two items:

• A brochure or flyer advertising the features of the culture
• A script for a television advertisement for the culture

---

a. When the teams have completed their work, have them make their presentations to the rest of the class as if they were salespersons from the travel agency.

SkyLight Training and Publishing Inc.

TRANSFER

STAGE IV

☛ The goal of the transfer section is to help students find the relevance of the lesson for their own lives. Here we want the lesson to extend beyond the lesson, into other curriculum areas, and finally into students' lives beyond the classroom.

The reflection on using cognitive organizers makes students aware of the patterns for thinking that were used in the lesson and that these same patterns can be employed elsewhere. Sharing what they learned with a partner brings to consciousness the key points of knowledge gained in the lesson. The reflective journal/log helps them make personal connections to and associations with the lesson.

1. Reflect on the lesson with the whole class, beginning with the use of the cognitive organizers.

   • Which of the three graphic organizers did you like most? Why?

   • Which did you like the least? Why?

   • What ideas do you have about other ways you could use these organizers in school (in this subject or another)?

2. Have students conclude the lesson by turning to a partner and discussing the following questions:

   • What new things did you learn about this culture?

   • What was exciting? surprising? distressing?

   • What would you say is this culture's greatest gift to our world today?

3. Finally have students write a reflection log entry that begins:

   I [would/would not] like to visit this culture someday because . . .

4. Ask volunteers to share what they wrote with the rest of the class.

SPIRAL ADAPTATIONS OF THE LESSON

Elementary School Level

1. Focus the lesson on understanding and appreciating the ethnic diversity represented in the class, or invite several persons from other cultures to visit the class.

2. Teach students how to use a simple matrix with the various cultures down the side of the matrix and the food, language, and family customs across the top.

MATRIX

	Food	Language	Customs
Mexican			
Korean			
German			
South African			

3. Have students fill in the boxes of the matrix with pictures from magazines and/or pictures they draw and color themselves.

Secondary School Level

1. Focus the lesson on comparing and contrasting key similarities and differences in the values, customs, and beliefs of three cultures.

2. Use the attribute web and classification chart (see blackline, p. 158), then introduce a three-way Venn diagram organizer for comparing and contrasting the cultures.

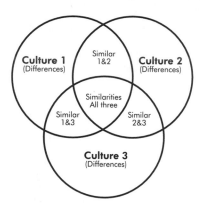

3. Role-play a debate on a contemporary issue with students assuming the values, beliefs, and customs of the different cultures in the discussion. For example, discuss the conflicts between technology and the environment, how to achieve world peace, or the pros and cons of a large family.

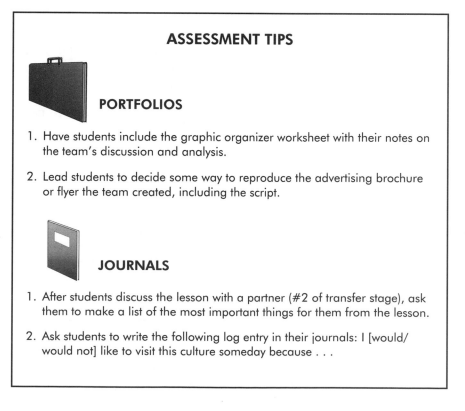

ASSESSMENT TIPS

PORTFOLIOS

1. Have students include the graphic organizer worksheet with their notes on the team's discussion and analysis.

2. Lead students to decide some way to reproduce the advertising brochure or flyer the team created, including the script.

JOURNALS

1. After students discuss the lesson with a partner (#2 of transfer stage), ask them to make a list of the most important things for them from the lesson.

2. Ask students to write the following log entry in their journals: I [would/would not] like to visit this culture someday because . . .

Look to the Past . . .

Rethink a lesson you have completed recently. How would you restructure it to teach *for* and *with* logical/mathematical intelligence?

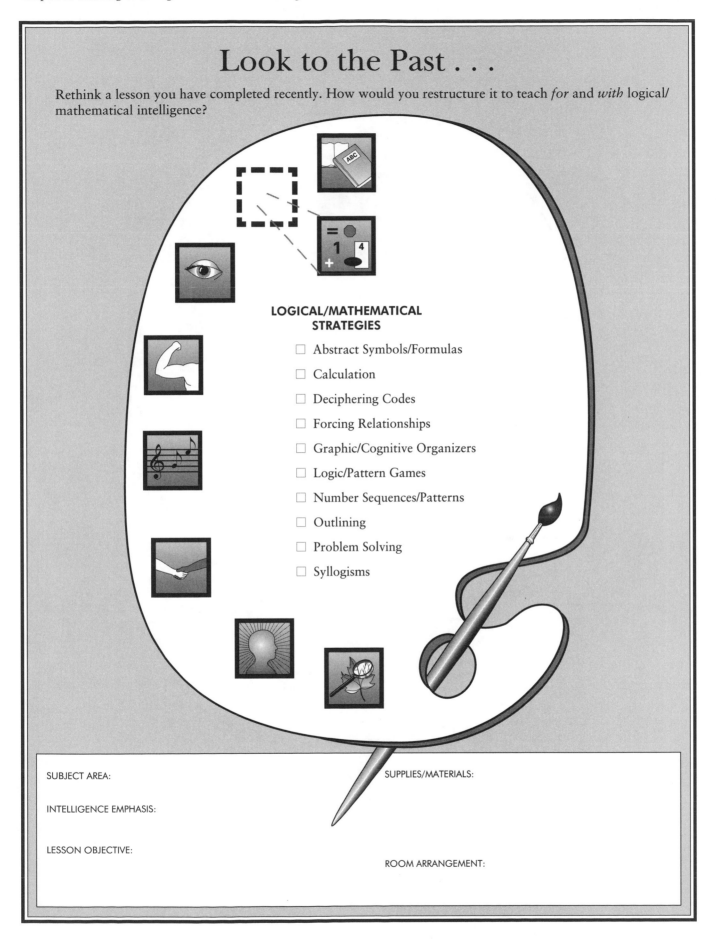

LOGICAL/MATHEMATICAL STRATEGIES

☐ Abstract Symbols/Formulas

☐ Calculation

☐ Deciphering Codes

☐ Forcing Relationships

☐ Graphic/Cognitive Organizers

☐ Logic/Pattern Games

☐ Number Sequences/Patterns

☐ Outlining

☐ Problem Solving

☐ Syllogisms

SUBJECT AREA:

INTELLIGENCE EMPHASIS:

LESSON OBJECTIVE:

SUPPLIES/MATERIALS:

ROOM ARRANGEMENT:

SkyLight Training and Publishing Inc.

Look to the Future . . .

Think about a lesson you have coming up in the near future. How would you structure it to teach *for* and *with* logical/mathematical intelligence?

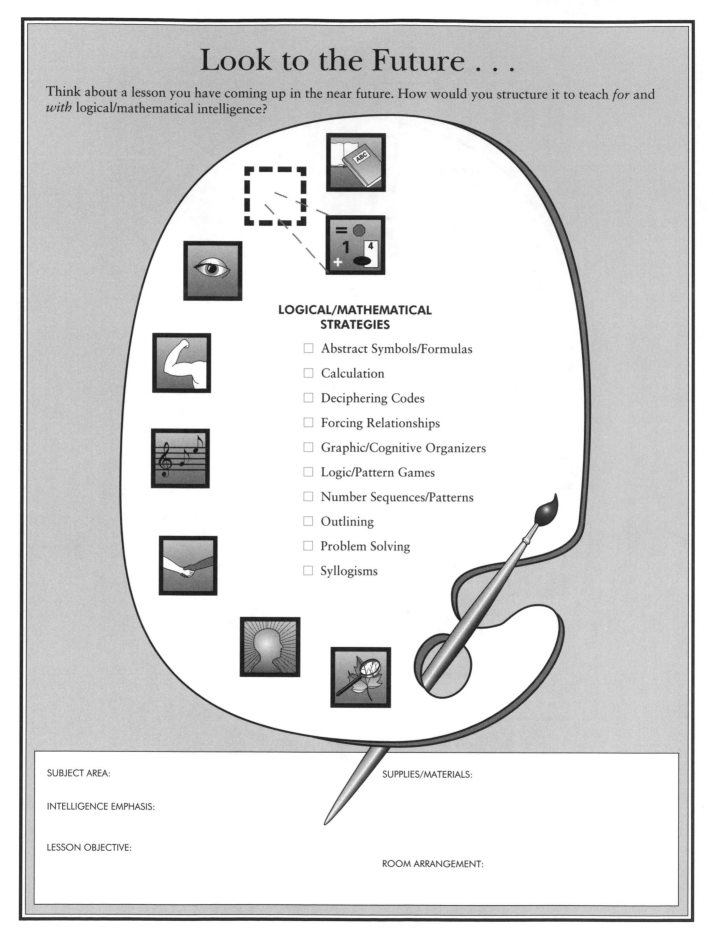

**LOGICAL/MATHEMATICAL
STRATEGIES**

- ☐ Abstract Symbols/Formulas
- ☐ Calculation
- ☐ Deciphering Codes
- ☐ Forcing Relationships
- ☐ Graphic/Cognitive Organizers
- ☐ Logic/Pattern Games
- ☐ Number Sequences/Patterns
- ☐ Outlining
- ☐ Problem Solving
- ☐ Syllogisms

SUBJECT AREA:

INTELLIGENCE EMPHASIS:

LESSON OBJECTIVE:

SUPPLIES/MATERIALS:

ROOM ARRANGEMENT:

Lesson Planning Ideas
Logical/Mathematical

HISTORY	MATHEMATICS	LANGUAGE ARTS	SCIENCE & HEALTH	GLOBAL STUDIES & GEOGRAPHY	FAMILY/CONSUMER SCIENCES, INDUSTRIAL TECHNOLOGY, & PE	FINE ARTS
Find examples when history repeated itself	Find unknown quantities or entities in a problem	Predict what will happen next in a story or play	Use the symbols of the Periodic Table of Elements in a story	Play Follow the Legend map-reading games and exercises	Follow a recipe to make bread from scratch	Learn patterns of ten different dance steps
Compare and contrast different periods of history	Teach someone else how to use a calculator for problem solving	Create a 4x4x4 outline** on a favorite hobby	Find five different ways to classify a collection of leaves	Play Guess the Culture based on artifacts in a time capsule	Find the relation of keyboard actions and computer performance	Compose a piece of music from a matrix**
Ask fat and skinny questions** about key historical decisions	Create number sequences and have a partner find the pattern	Learn to read, write, and decipher code language	Do a KWL goal-setting chart** for a study of AIDS	Rank-order key socioeconomic factors that shaped a culture	Design a physical exercise routine using a matrix**	Use a Venn diagram** to analyze characters in a play
Create time sequence charts with titles for major eras of history	Mind-map* proofs for geometry theorems	Analyze similarities and differences of various pieces of literature	Learn the pattern of successful and reliable scientific experiments	Predict what will happen in several current event stories	Create problem-solving scenarios for shop machines	Create a paint-by-numbers picture for another person to paint
Predict what the next decade will be like based on patterns of the past	Design classification charts for math formulas and operations	Use a story grid** for creative writing activities	Practice webbing** attributes of various systems of the body	Learn cause and effect relations of geography and geological events	Make a matrix* on meanings of computer symbols	Analyze plays using the dramatic structure model*

* See Glossary
** See Glossary and Appendix C

CHAPTER

3

TEACHING WITH
VISUAL/SPATIAL
INTELLIGENCE

THE INCREDIBLE JOURNEY
OF PHOTOSYNTHESIS

A Biology Lesson:

Secondary School Level

SkyLight Training and Publishing Inc.

Lesson Palette: *Visual/Spatial* Emphasis

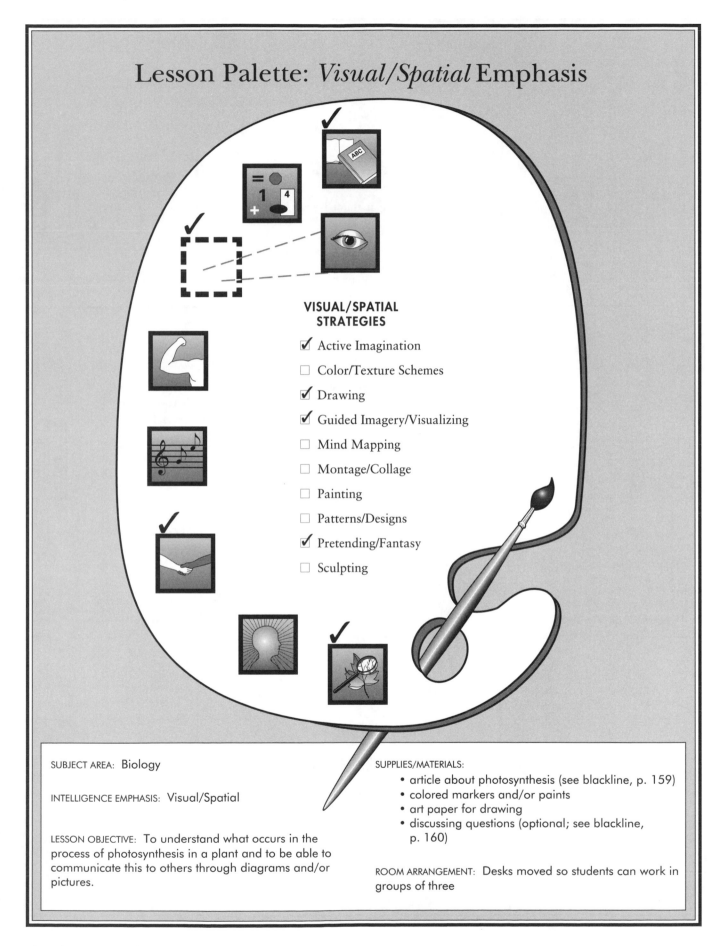

VISUAL/SPATIAL STRATEGIES

- ☑ Active Imagination
- ☐ Color/Texture Schemes
- ☑ Drawing
- ☑ Guided Imagery/Visualizing
- ☐ Mind Mapping
- ☐ Montage/Collage
- ☐ Painting
- ☐ Patterns/Designs
- ☑ Pretending/Fantasy
- ☐ Sculpting

SUBJECT AREA: Biology

INTELLIGENCE EMPHASIS: Visual/Spatial

LESSON OBJECTIVE: To understand what occurs in the process of photosynthesis in a plant and to be able to communicate this to others through diagrams and/or pictures.

SUPPLIES/MATERIALS:
- article about photosynthesis (see blackline, p. 159)
- colored markers and/or paints
- art paper for drawing
- discussing questions (optional; see blackline, p. 160)

ROOM ARRANGEMENT: Desks moved so students can work in groups of three

THE LESSON . . .

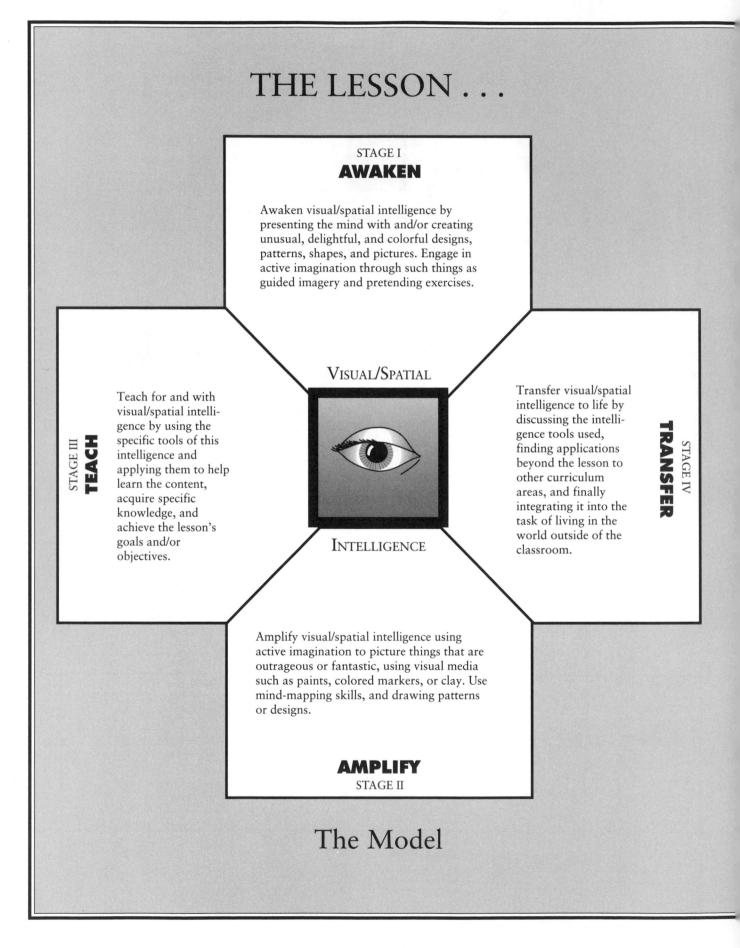

STAGE I
AWAKEN

Awaken visual/spatial intelligence by presenting the mind with and/or creating unusual, delightful, and colorful designs, patterns, shapes, and pictures. Engage in active imagination through such things as guided imagery and pretending exercises.

VISUAL/SPATIAL

STAGE III
TEACH

Teach for and with visual/spatial intelligence by using the specific tools of this intelligence and applying them to help learn the content, acquire specific knowledge, and achieve the lesson's goals and/or objectives.

STAGE IV
TRANSFER

Transfer visual/spatial intelligence to life by discussing the intelligence tools used, finding applications beyond the lesson to other curriculum areas, and finally integrating it into the task of living in the world outside of the classroom.

INTELLIGENCE

Amplify visual/spatial intelligence using active imagination to picture things that are outrageous or fantastic, using visual media such as paints, colored markers, or clay. Use mind-mapping skills, and drawing patterns or designs.

AMPLIFY
STAGE II

The Model

SkyLight Training and Publishing Inc.

...AT A GLANCE

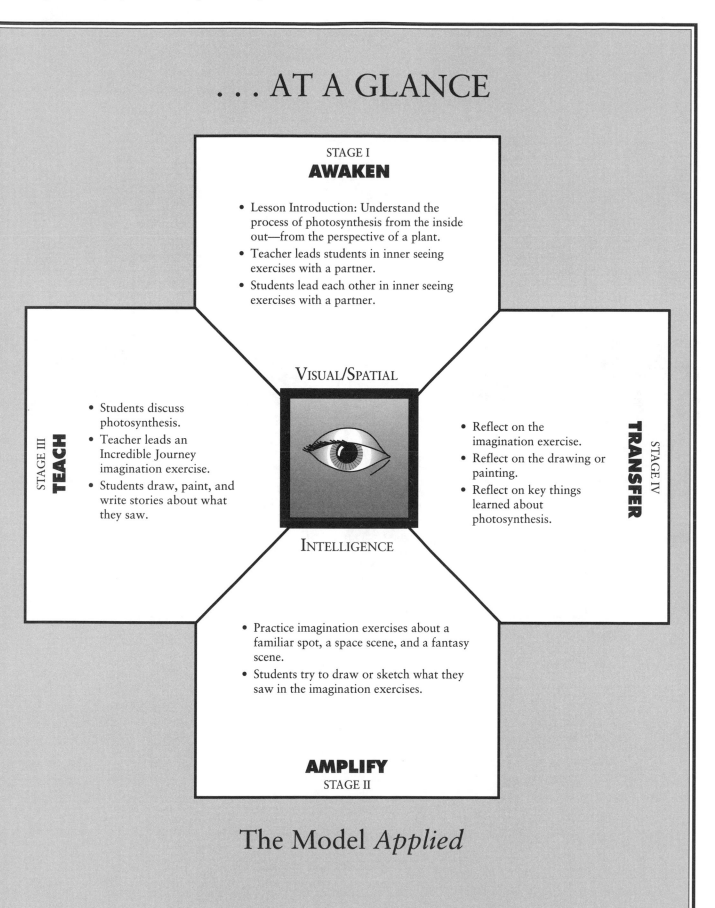

STAGE I
AWAKEN

- Lesson Introduction: Understand the process of photosynthesis from the inside out—from the perspective of a plant.
- Teacher leads students in inner seeing exercises with a partner.
- Students lead each other in inner seeing exercises with a partner.

VISUAL/SPATIAL

STAGE III
TEACH

- Students discuss photosynthesis.
- Teacher leads an Incredible Journey imagination exercise.
- Students draw, paint, and write stories about what they saw.

STAGE IV
TRANSFER

- Reflect on the imagination exercise.
- Reflect on the drawing or painting.
- Reflect on key things learned about photosynthesis.

INTELLIGENCE

- Practice imagination exercises about a familiar spot, a space scene, and a fantasy scene.
- Students try to draw or sketch what they saw in the imagination exercises.

AMPLIFY
STAGE II

The Model *Applied*

SkyLight Training and Publishing Inc.

The Incredible Journey
of Photosynthesis

A Biology Lesson with

Visual/Spatial Intelligence

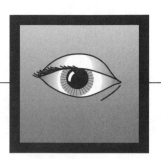

Lesson Procedures

☛ The realm of visual/spatial intelligence is the realm of images, patterns, colors, designs, textures, pictures, and the like. The process of seeing something with the external eyes (mostly from the stimulation of the retina) activates the visual area of the brain. In the case of visual/spatial intelligence, we are mostly dealing with a right-brain hemispheric operation—an area known as the parietal lobes (see fig. 0.5, p.12). When sets of neural pathways fire, we experience an image. Researchers have found that the firing of these neural pathways can also be caused by internal stimulation. Many of the same physical operations present in normal, external eye perception are likewise present in mental imagery, when one is seeing with the mind's eye. Often the mere creation of a strong mental image will cause us to react as if the imagined thing is real.

INTRODUCTION

The natural world is an awesome miracle if we but open our eyes and see. In this lesson students have an opportunity to explore and understand the process of photosynthesis in a unique way—from the inside out; that is, from the perspective of the plant! The lesson is modeled after the movie *The Incredible Journey* where human beings became microscopic and traveled through the body in the bloodstream. In this lesson, students imagine that they can journey into a plant and participate in the amazing photosynthesis process. They will be using their visual/spatial intelligence in the lesson so ask them to be aware of this and notice what happens.

In addition to visual/spatial intelligence, this lesson employs verbal/linguistic, interpersonal, and naturalist intelligence. The verbal/linguistic emphasis can be seen in the writing students do in the transfer section of the lesson. The interpersonal emphasis is in the cooperative group work students do throughout the lesson. The naturalist intelligence is used when the students visualize a plant.

STAGE I

☛ Visual/spatial intelligence is awakened by presenting the mind with unusual, delightful, and colorful designs, patterns, shapes, and pictures, and engaging in active imagination through such things as imagination and pretending exercises.

AWAKEN

1. Tell students you are going to ask them to see various things with the mind's eye, and that you are going to help them access and turn on the parts of the brain that will help them do this. Ask students to find a partner, put their heads together, and close their eyes. Tell students that you are going to suggest a series of images to them and they are to tell their partner what they see

When you engage in this kind of image association, the visual part of the brain immediately creates pictures, memories, emotions, and other sensations that it connects with the image suggested. Not only do the students see their own associations, but they also receive further image input as their partners describe their respective associations. When you have completed the image associations, just listen to the buzz that will be present in the room!

with the mind's eye. (Note: This is like a word association test but with images instead.) Suggest these images:

- an animal
- a machine
- a park
- a storm
- an elderly person
- a trip
- a food
- a relative
- swimming
- a party
- yourself as a baby
- shopping

2. Have students discuss the process of inner seeing with each other. Prompt them to ask each other What happened? and What was this like?

3. Ask several partners to share some of their observations with the whole class.

STAGE II

☞ One of the key findings of researchers is that, although one or two of our intellectual capacities tends to be more developed than the others, they can all be strengthened and improved. This is especially true of our visual/spatial potentials. When we were much younger our visual/spatial capacities were generally very strong and often second nature to us in daydreaming, pretending, and role playing. However, as we get older, we are told that this world of active imagination is only for children, so we tend to use these capacities less and less. Nevertheless, contemporary research has documented that the capacity for imagination is inherent in the nervous system, and thus can be relearned and improved.

Here students imagine a familiar scene and then sketch on paper what they have seen inside their heads. Remember, this is not an art lesson! It is therefore important to emphasize that whatever they are seeing is fine and however they represent on their papers what they are seeing is perfectly acceptable.

 **AMPLIFY**

1. Tell students that in their biology lesson today they will be participating in an imagination exercise and that they will sketch what they have seen using the mind's eye. But first lead them in a few practice imagination exercises so they have an understanding of the basic process.

2. Pass out blank paper and colored pencils or markers to students. Students are to work individually this time. Instruct them to try to imagine as vividly as possible the things you are going to suggest to them.

3. Begin by having them close their eyes, take several deep breaths, and relax as much as they can. After a couple of minutes, give these instructions:

   a. Now I'd like you to imagine that you are in your bedroom at home. Look around and try to see as much as you can with your mind's eye. (pause)

   b. Notice whether or not the bed is made. (pause)

   c. Are any clothes lying out? How light is it? Notice any other special things in the room. (pause)

   d. Now on a sheet of blank paper, briefly draw or sketch what you are seeing in your mind's eye.

4. Have students share their drawings and talk about the imagination exercise with their partners.

5. Tell students that you want them to practice this once again, but this time they will have to use their imagination even more, because you will be taking them on a journey to an unfamiliar place. Again ask them to close their eyes and relax, breathing

☞ The purpose of the second imagination exercise is to help students practice using their imagination more fully by imagining an unfamiliar scene. Granted, they are likely to draw pictures they have seen of outer space, but their active imagination must fill in the gaps and this is point of the exercise. This practice is important for it is more akin to the photosynthesis journey on which you take them later in the lesson.

☞ It is important to recognize that there are no wrong answers in an imagination exercise. Whatever happens, whatever they experience is right! Make sure students are aware of this.

STAGE III

☞ The traditional academic content part of the lesson can either be a review of previously studied material, or it could be an introduction to a more in-depth study of photosynthesis.

Whether you use the article provided or another from your own biology textbook is not important. (If you do use a different article, you will need to make alterations in the guided imagery instructions so they match the article the students have studied.) The purpose of reading the article is for students to have the basic stages of the photosynthesis process in a fairly concise form, for it is these stages that will be the stages of the guided imagery journey on which you take them after their initial study. At this point you are also accessing both verbal/linguistic intelligence through the reading and discussion, and interpersonal intelligence in and through the cooperative group structure.

☞ For many students, especially those who have a more fully developed naturalist intelligence, the visualization may stimulate and trigger this intelligence within them. What you are attempting to do, in any event, is create a virtual experience of nature by asking students to vividly and actively imagine a plant.

SkyLight Training and Publishing Inc.

deeply from the abdomen. After a couple of minutes suggest the following images to the students:

a. Imagine that you are lying down in a favorite outdoor place of yours. Take a couple of moments to think of that place and then, as vividly as you can, imagine that you are there. (pause)

b. Imagine that you are lying there, completely relaxed, and enjoying yourself, and that you are able to slowly float upwards into the clouds. Let yourself do that now. Try to notice everything you can about what this is like. (pause)

c. Now imagine that you can continue to float higher and higher until you leave the atmosphere of the earth and you find yourself in space. Spend a few minutes looking around and getting a sense of what space is like. (pause)

d. When you feel ready, allow yourself to float back into the earth's atmosphere, into the clouds, and back to the favorite spot where you began. (pause)

e. Now open your eyes and quickly sketch what you saw and experienced on your trip to space on a piece of blank paper.

6. Once again have students briefly share their drawings and their experience of the imagination exercise with their partners.

 **TEACH**

1. Have students get into cooperative groups of three. Assign the roles of organizer, encourager, and checker. Have the organizer gather supplies for the team: colored markers or pencils, blank paper, and a copy of the the article on photosynthesis (see blackline, p. 159).

2. Instruct students to read the article as a team and answer the discussion questions (see blackline, p. 160). Tell them that they are to help each other understand the process; that is, what happens during photosynthesis.

3. Now tell the class that they are going to have a chance to experience the process of photosynthesis. Ask if any of the students have seen the movie *The Incredible Journey*. If so, have them tell the story to the rest of the class. If not, tell it yourself (see lesson introduction above). Explain that students are going to take an incredible journey into a plant and experience the process of photosynthesis firsthand.

4. Introduce the process by telling the students that you are going to lead them in an imagination exercise as you did earlier.

a. Ask them to think about some of the things that are in a factory, such as machines, an energy supply, workers, a water supply, etc. Tell them they are to imagine that the leaf is a

☞ It is very important that you find ways to help students get into the imagination exercise. We all imagine things in our mind's eye, but not in the same way. Some students will see in their minds with the same clarity that they see television. Others will only have a vague impression of what you are suggesting. Still others may see nothing at all in the traditional sense of seeing, but may have an inner feeling for what you are suggesting. In any guided imagery, success is whatever works for the individual. There is no right way! If the images suggested are not working, give students permission to cheat! Have them pretend it is working, or even better, tell them they can change the images for themselves so they do work. With practice, inner seeing can be improved.

☞ Doing the exercise with eyes closed generally helps the active imagination work better. It also helps students stay focused on the journey and not get distracted. However, if any are uncomfortable with closing their eyes, make sure they know they can keep them open. But ask them to experiment with closed eyes if they want.

small photosynthesis factory. Tell them that you will be taking them on a tour of this factory so they can see and experience the stages of photosynthesis they have just been reading about.

b. Tell them you will pause after each stage of the tour and give them a chance to briefly sketch what they are seeing in their mind's eye on a piece of paper.

c. Explain that at the end of the tour the team will look at the different pictures individuals have drawn and incorporate different individual pictures into a single picture of the photosynthesis process. Encourage students to let their minds run wild and see how much they can get into this journey.

5. Now begin the process by asking students to close their eyes. Instruct them to breathe deeply and relax as much as possible for a few minutes. When you sense they are ready, lead them in the process outlined below. Read the following instructions to the class:

a. Imagine that you are in the middle of a beautiful, green woods. It is a gorgeous spring day and the warm sun is shining brightly above. (pause)

b. Pretend that you have the power to make yourself much, much smaller than you are now. Maybe you do this as the characters did in *The Incredible Journey* movie by drinking some special drink, or maybe there is a special seed you eat, or you may have some other way to do this. But now I'd like you to make yourself very, very tiny. In fact, I'd like you to make yourself so small that you become microscopic. I'll now give you a few minutes to do this by whatever means you choose. (pause)

c. You have now become so small that you are able to walk through a pore in the leaf of a nearby plant. As you enter the plant you suddenly find yourself surrounded by hundreds of thousands of cells. As you look more closely at one of the cells you notice that it is like a little factory. There is a supply of water flowing through it from the veins of the plant. There is an acceptor module (like a special chamber in the factory) that is gathering carbon dioxide as it enters the plant through the pores in the leaf.

d. Now, open your eyes and briefly sketch a cell as if it were a factory. Include the water supply, the carbon dioxide acceptor chamber (molecule), and anything else you are seeing or sensing. What does look like? (pause)

e. Close your eyes again. As you continue walking around this cell, you notice a football-shaped, green plate that seems to be seeking out and turning in the direction of the sunlight that is striking the surface of the leaf. You remember from your reading that this is the chloroplast. It is the light radar system of the plant and it can move to take best advantage of the light.

f. Pause for a moment again and add the chloroplast light radar system to your picture. What does this look like in your mind's eye? (pause)

g. As you look more closely at the cell you notice that there are many chloroplast light radar stations stacked on top of each other. In between the chloroplasts is a green, sponge-like substance that you suddenly know is the chlorophyll molecules—the plant's light absorbing unit. You notice the chlorophyll molecules soaking up the sunlight. Again, pause for a moment and draw what you are seeing. (pause)

h. Now close your eyes again. You hear the sound of water and notice that it is flowing into the cell from the veins of the leaf. Pause and add this to your picture. (pause)

i. Close your eyes again. Focus again on the chlorophyll. You suddenly become aware that the chlorophyll molecules are much more than sun-sucking sponges. They are like little reactors in and of themselves. As they get more and more charged with energy from the sun, they begin to split the water molecules flowing through the cell into hydrogen and oxygen. The oxygen is expelled back into the atmosphere through the pores of the leaf and the hydrogen atoms are seized by a special escort module and held in a special place for later in the process. Open your eyes and draw what you are seeing— the chlorophyll splitting the water molecule, the oxygen being expelled, and the hydrogen being held by the escort module. (pause)

j. Close your eyes again. Once the chlorophyll has split the water molecules, it gives off more energy as it returns to its normal state. This energy, however, turns on a new molecule, the ATP. ATP is like an electric generator that empowers the escort module that is holding on to the hydrogen atom. Pause now and sketch this image. (pause)

k. The escort module now leads the hydrogen to the carbon dioxide acceptor module and they combine to form PGA molecules. These PGA molecules combine with each other to form sugar, and the sugar is placed in storage areas in the plant to be used later for food. For the last time now, pause and draw what this part of process looks like to you in your mind's eye. (pause)

l. The process is now complete. Pause for a moment and allow yourself to appreciate what you have just experienced. Reflect on the amazing process of photosynthesis in this microscopic factory that makes food from sunlight. (pause)

m. Now, as you are ready, find your way back to the pore in the leaf of the plant where you originally entered and exit to the place where you began. Slowly allow yourself to become your normal size again, by whatever means you choose. (pause)

n. As you are ready, bring yourself back to this room, and to this time and space. Open your eyes and stretch, looking at your picture of the photosynthesis factory, remembering the journey in which you have been participating.

6. Now give time for each student to share his or her picture with the other members of the team.

7. Pass out poster paper and colored markers to each team and have them create a single picture of a photosynthesis factory based on the ideas from the different pictures the individual members of the team have drawn. Make sure they know that they are to include ideas from each member of the team and that you want the individual pictures attached to the final product so you can check to make sure each person has contributed to the final drawing.

8. Have three teams get together and share their final pictures with each other. Note similarities and differences in the pictures of the factories.

☛ Every idea of each individual does not need to to be included in the final picture, but you want some of the ideas from each member of the team to be included in the final product.

TRANSFER

STAGE IV

☛ The goal of the transfer part of the lesson is to help students take what they have learned in the lesson and apply it in other areas of their schoolwork and in their everyday lives outside of school.

Reflecting on the process serves two metacognitive functions: it helps students be more aware of their own visual/spatial intelligence capacities and helps them think about how these capacities can be improved. The reflective log/journal writing allows students to distill the key points of the lesson for themselves in language and terminology that makes sense to them.

If you like, use the Discussion Questions blackline (p. 160) to process the lesson with the entire class.

1. Reflect on the imagination exercise with the students using the following questions:

   • What happened in the imagination exercise? What what was it like for you?

   • What surprised you? What was exciting? What was difficult?

   • How was this imaginary journey different from just reading about photosynthesis?

   • What new things did it add to your understanding?

2. Reflect on the learnings from the content part of the lesson.

   a. Ask students to write a reflection in their logs describing their journey into the cell factory of the plant. The log is to be titled, A Day in the Life of a Plant Cell.

   b. Ask for volunteers to share something from their log entry.

SPIRAL ADAPTATIONS OF THE LESSON

Elementary School Level

1. Focus the lesson on understanding the different parts of a plant and the function each part performs (e.g., the roots absorb water and nutrients from the earth, the leaves soak up sunshine from which the plant makes its food, etc.).

2. Have students draw pictures of plants showing all of the different parts discussed above. Then let them paint their pictures with watercolors. You could also have them make a plant from clay.

3. Ask students to pretend they can talk to their plant and ask it questions about what it is like to be a plant. Pretend that the plant can answer. Let the plant ask the students questions about what it is like to be human.

Middle School Level

1. Focus the lesson on learning about the life of a plant that is beyond what the naked eye can see (e.g., pores in a leaf, the different kinds of cells that make up a plant, the tiny veins, etc.).

2. Have students observe differents parts of plants under a microscope and draw what they are seeing on paper using colored markers and/or pencils.

3. Place students in cooperative groups and have them paint a large mural that shows the inner aspects of the life of a plant and incorporates the different things they have seen under the microscope. The murals are to tell the story of the life of a plant from the inside out.

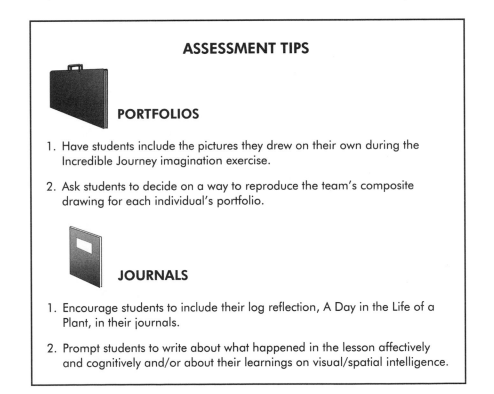

ASSESSMENT TIPS

PORTFOLIOS

1. Have students include the pictures they drew on their own during the Incredible Journey imagination exercise.

2. Ask students to decide on a way to reproduce the team's composite drawing for each individual's portfolio.

JOURNALS

1. Encourage students to include their log reflection, A Day in the Life of a Plant, in their journals.

2. Prompt students to write about what happened in the lesson affectively and cognitively and/or about their learnings on visual/spatial intelligence.

Look to the Past . . .

Rethink a lesson you have completed recently. How would you restructure it to teach *for* and *with* visual/spatial intelligence?

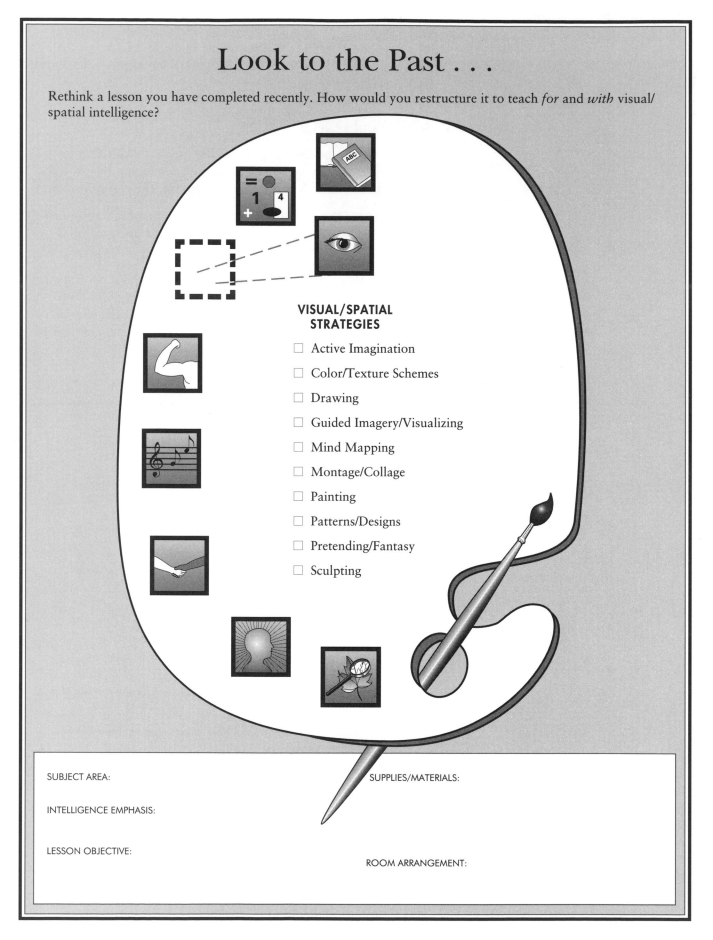

VISUAL/SPATIAL STRATEGIES

- ☐ Active Imagination
- ☐ Color/Texture Schemes
- ☐ Drawing
- ☐ Guided Imagery/Visualizing
- ☐ Mind Mapping
- ☐ Montage/Collage
- ☐ Painting
- ☐ Patterns/Designs
- ☐ Pretending/Fantasy
- ☐ Sculpting

SUBJECT AREA:

INTELLIGENCE EMPHASIS:

LESSON OBJECTIVE:

SUPPLIES/MATERIALS:

ROOM ARRANGEMENT:

Look to the Future . . .

Think about a lesson you have coming up in the near future. How would you structure it to teach *for* and *with* visual/spatial intelligence?

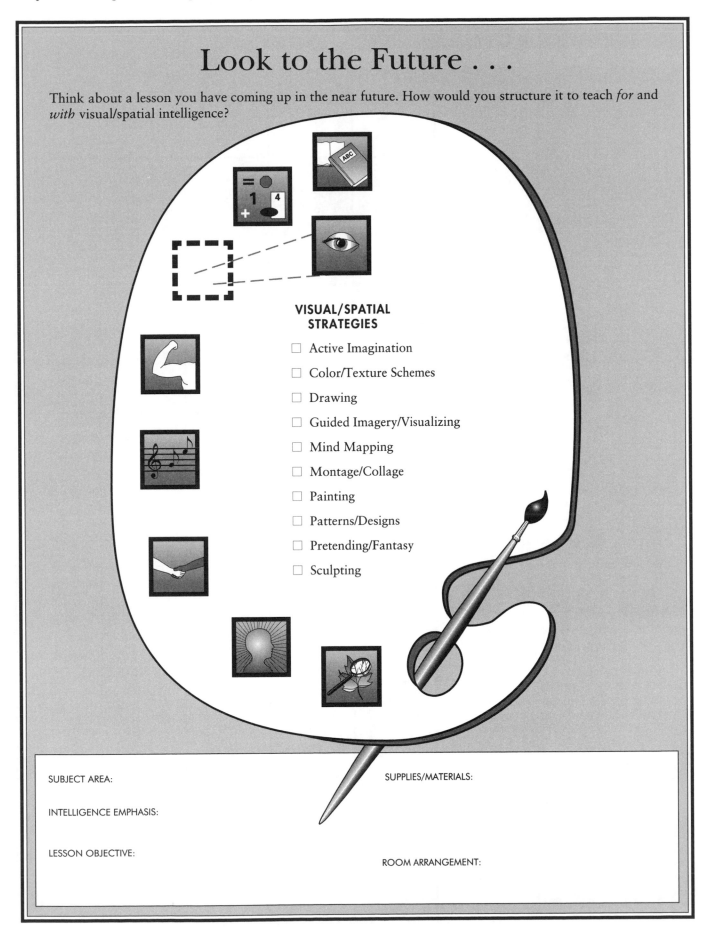

VISUAL/SPATIAL STRATEGIES

- ☐ Active Imagination
- ☐ Color/Texture Schemes
- ☐ Drawing
- ☐ Guided Imagery/Visualizing
- ☐ Mind Mapping
- ☐ Montage/Collage
- ☐ Painting
- ☐ Patterns/Designs
- ☐ Pretending/Fantasy
- ☐ Sculpting

SUBJECT AREA:

INTELLIGENCE EMPHASIS:

LESSON OBJECTIVE:

SUPPLIES/MATERIALS:

ROOM ARRANGEMENT:

LESSON PLANNING IDEAS
Visual/Spatial

HISTORY	MATHEMATICS	LANGUAGE ARTS	SCIENCE & HEALTH	GLOBAL STUDIES & GEOGRAPHY	FAMILY/CONSUMER SCIENCES, INDUSTRIAL TECHNOLOGY, & PE	FINE ARTS
Have imaginary talks or interviews with people from the past	Do a survey of students' likes and dislikes, then graph the results	Play Pictionary with vocabulary words	Draw pictures of things seen under a microscope	Draw maps of the world from your visual memory	Draw pictures of how to perform certain physical feats	Watch dancers on video and imagine yourself in their shoes
Make visual diagrams and flowcharts of historical facts	Estimate measurements by sight and by touch	Use mind mapping* as a notetaking process	Create posters or flyers showing healthy eating practices	Study a culture through its visual art—painting and sculpture	Create visual diagrams of how to use shop machines	Pretend you can enter a painting—imagine what it is like
Imagine going back in time—see what it was like back then	Add, subtract, multiply, and divide using various manipulatives	Draw pictures of the different stages of a story you are reading	Create montages or collages on science topics (e.g., mammals)	Make maps out of clay and show geographical features	Practice drawing objects from different angles (drafting)	Listen to music with eyes closed and create a sculpture from clay
Paint a mural about a period of history	Imagine using a math process successfully, then really do it	Learn to read, write, and decipher code language	Draw visual patterns that appear in the natural world	Make decor for the classroom on a culture you are studying	Learn a series of spatial games (e.g., horseshoes, ring toss)	Draw the sets for the various scenes of a play you are reading
Imagine and draw what you think the future will be like	Learn metric measurement through visual equivalents	Use highlight markers to colorize parts of a story or poem	Pretend you are microscopic and can travel in the bloodstream	Use a map to get around an unfamiliar place or location	Imagine your computer is human—draw how it works	Draw the visual and color pattern of a dance

*See Glossary

SkyLight Training and Publishing Inc.

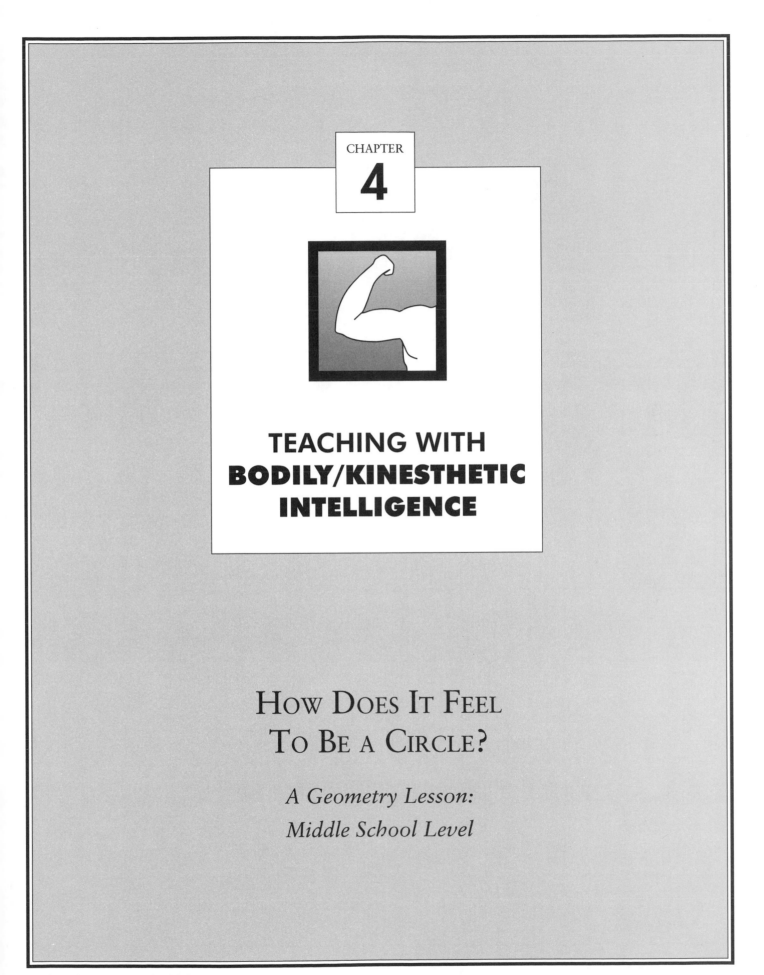

TEACHING WITH BODILY/KINESTHETIC INTELLIGENCE

HOW DOES IT FEEL
TO BE A CIRCLE?

A Geometry Lesson:
Middle School Level

SkyLight Training and Publishing Inc.

Lesson Palette: *Bodily/Kinesthetic* Emphasis

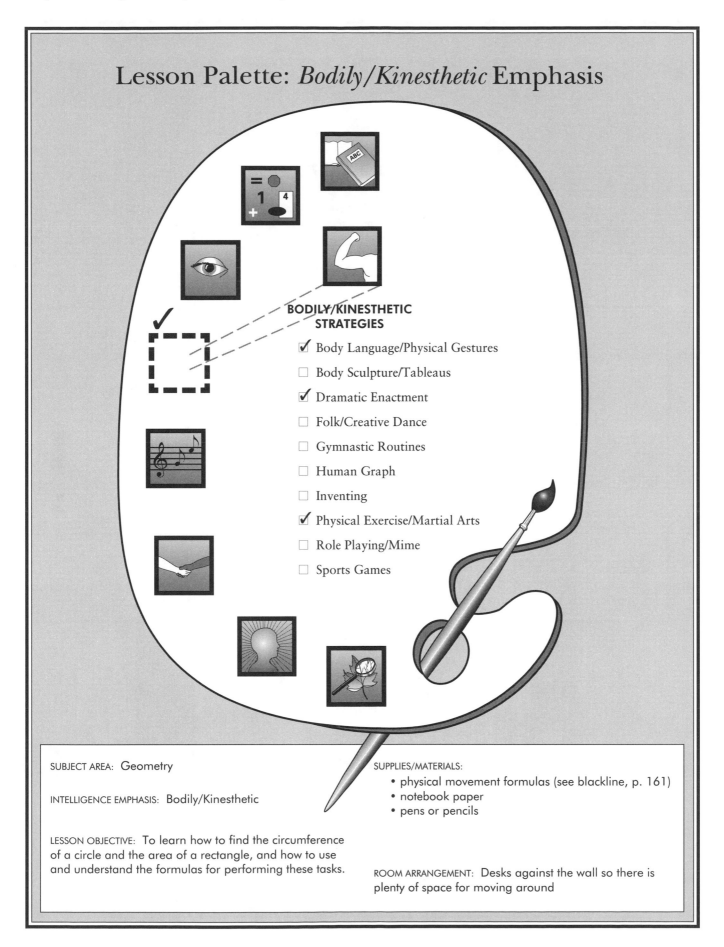

BODILY/KINESTHETIC STRATEGIES

- ☑ Body Language/Physical Gestures
- ☐ Body Sculpture/Tableaus
- ☑ Dramatic Enactment
- ☐ Folk/Creative Dance
- ☐ Gymnastic Routines
- ☐ Human Graph
- ☐ Inventing
- ☑ Physical Exercise/Martial Arts
- ☐ Role Playing/Mime
- ☐ Sports Games

SUBJECT AREA: Geometry

INTELLIGENCE EMPHASIS: Bodily/Kinesthetic

LESSON OBJECTIVE: To learn how to find the circumference of a circle and the area of a rectangle, and how to use and understand the formulas for performing these tasks.

SUPPLIES/MATERIALS:
- physical movement formulas (see blackline, p. 161)
- notebook paper
- pens or pencils

ROOM ARRANGEMENT: Desks against the wall so there is plenty of space for moving around

THE LESSON . . .

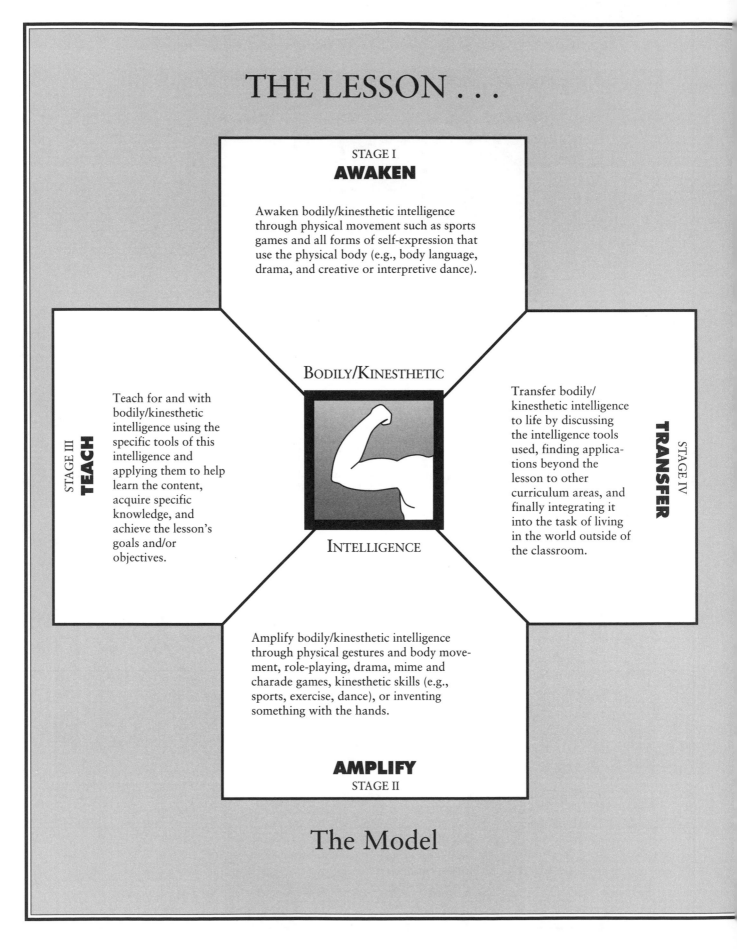

STAGE I

AWAKEN

Awaken bodily/kinesthetic intelligence through physical movement such as sports games and all forms of self-expression that use the physical body (e.g., body language, drama, and creative or interpretive dance).

BODILY/KINESTHETIC

STAGE III TEACH

Teach for and with bodily/kinesthetic intelligence using the specific tools of this intelligence and applying them to help learn the content, acquire specific knowledge, and achieve the lesson's goals and/or objectives.

STAGE IV TRANSFER

Transfer bodily/kinesthetic intelligence to life by discussing the intelligence tools used, finding applications beyond the lesson to other curriculum areas, and finally integrating it into the task of living in the world outside of the classroom.

INTELLIGENCE

Amplify bodily/kinesthetic intelligence through physical gestures and body movement, role-playing, drama, mime and charade games, kinesthetic skills (e.g., sports, exercise, dance), or inventing something with the hands.

AMPLIFY

STAGE II

The Model

SkyLight Training and Publishing Inc.

. . . AT A GLANCE

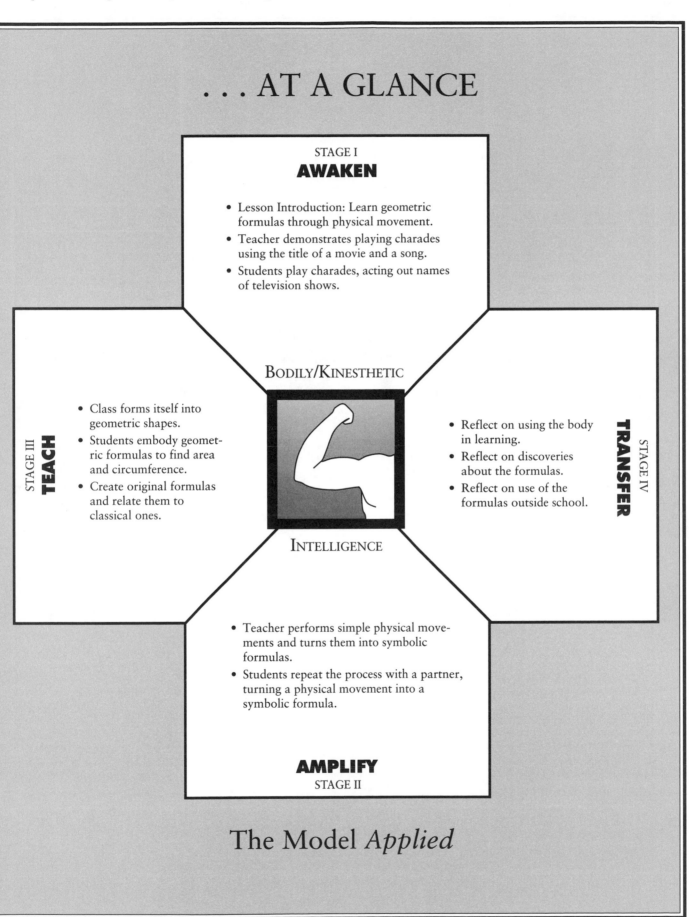

STAGE I
AWAKEN

- Lesson Introduction: Learn geometric formulas through physical movement.
- Teacher demonstrates playing charades using the title of a movie and a song.
- Students play charades, acting out names of television shows.

BODILY/KINESTHETIC

INTELLIGENCE

STAGE III
TEACH

- Class forms itself into geometric shapes.
- Students embody geometric formulas to find area and circumference.
- Create original formulas and relate them to classical ones.

STAGE IV
TRANSFER

- Reflect on using the body in learning.
- Reflect on discoveries about the formulas.
- Reflect on use of the formulas outside school.

- Teacher performs simple physical movements and turns them into symbolic formulas.
- Students repeat the process with a partner, turning a physical movement into a symbolic formula.

AMPLIFY
STAGE II

The Model *Applied*

How Does It Feel To
Be a Circle?

A GEOMETRY LESSON WITH

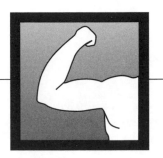

Bodily/Kinesthetic Intelligence

Lesson Procedures

INTRODUCTION

In this lesson students will learn two different geometric formulas by physically "embodying" them. They will learn the formulas with their bodies, create their own formulas to describe the physical movements they have made, and finally transfer this learning to the classical geometric formulas. Tell the students that this lesson will emphasize bodily/kinesthetic intelligence as the primary way of knowing. Ask them to be aware of this as they work.

Two other intelligences are also used in this lesson. Logical/mathematical intelligence is involved when students recognize patterns, in this case physical movement patterns, and convert these patterns into abstract symbolic formulas. Interpersonal intelligence is involved as students work with a partner to create their formulas.

 **AWAKEN**

Begin by playing charades with the class:

1. Think of a movie that most students have seen and the name of a popular song they know. Act out clues to the various words in the movie title while students guess. After they have succeeded in guessing the movie title, act out the song title.

2. Now break the class into teams of three. Have the teams play charades with each other by drawing the names of current television shows from a hat and acting out their titles for each other.

☛ Bodily/kinesthetic capacities involve a set of highly complex brain, mind, and body operations. We know that the right side of the brain controls the motor functions of the left side of the body, and the left side of the brain controls the right side of the body. The cerebral cortex of the brain (see fig. 0.5, p.12) is like a radar system that continually monitors and interprets the meaning of various data all over the body. This information is fed to the cerebral cortex through the spinal cord. Once the cerebral cortex has this information and has processed and interpreted it, the motor cortex kicks into gear, and produces the bodily movement needed to respond to what the cerebral cortex has discerned. All of this happens in a split second!

___

STAGE I

___

☛ The very act of physical movement creates an immense amount of activity in the brain. When you add to this the necessity to communicate in and through that movement, the fullness of the body as a vehicle of expression and/or knowing is activated.

For centuries people have understood that there are things that can be known and expressed physically that cannot be known or expressed in any other way—consider the world's rich traditions of drama, creative dance, mime, various cultural festivals, and religious pageantry. When you ask students to act out something, you call all of this potency to the foreground so that you can use it in the rest of the lesson.

___

STAGE II

☛ It is often easier to understand the need to practice body movement skills than it is to understand the need to practice some of the other intelligences. This is most likely because our culture is very much aware of the training athletes go through to compete in sports events. We know that through careful and regular practice we can improve such things as our serve in tennis, our skill in ice skating, and the ability to parallel park. There are many things that our bodies know that are not necessarily clear to the mind, such as how to ride a bike, how to type without looking at the keyboard, how to ski, and how to walk without toppling over.

☛ The teacher first models the skill that the students later employ in the lesson. It is important that the modeling be as close as possible to what you are actually going to have them do in the lesson. However, the more content-free the demonstration is the more students will be able to focus on learning the skill itself without being distracted by other information.

☛ Students need a chance to experience what it is like to learn and know things with the body, especially in the classroom where they are generally asked to leave their bodies outside! Here they are given an opportunity to practice creating physical movement formulas of their own as you modeled earlier.

Allow three rounds so that each student gets a chance to act out a title.

AMPLIFY

1. Introduce the intelligence skill by putting the following formulas on the board or overhead and see if students can guess what the formulas represent (see blackline, p. 161).

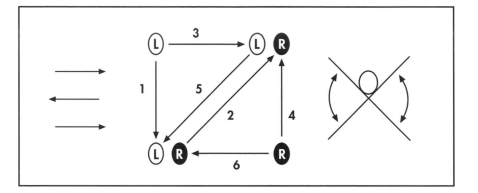

After they have had a few minutes to guess, tell them they are formulas that symbolize different kinds of physical movement. Perform the three different movements (#1—walking back and forth across the room, #2—the box step, #3—a jumping jack) and see if they can guess which movement goes with which formula. Help them see the relationship between the various parts of the formula and the movement it represents.

2. Working in the same groups of three in which they played charades, have students draw an item out of a hat. This time they will get a physical movement they are to perform as a team and then turn it into a symbolic formula as you have demonstrated above. Remind them that they are learning how to do this in order to use this skill later in the lesson. (Note: Items in the hat might include doing five push ups, moving from your desk to sharpen your pencil and back to your desk, throwing a piece of paper into the trash can, etc.)

☞ This is a process of translating physical movements into symbolic formulas of students' own creation, this time to learn geometry concepts. It gives students an opportunity to experience the relationship between their movements and an abstract formula that symbolizes the movement.

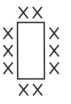 **TEACH**

1. The first task is to find the area of a rectangle. Have ten students volunteer to form a rectangle having the width of four students and the length of five students. Give them a rope to stretch around the inside of the rectangle they have formed.

```
      X X
   X      X
   X      X
   X      X
      X X
```

2. Ask the class to guess how many students it will take to fill in the rectangle. Record these estimates on the board or overhead.

3. Now have the students one by one enter the rectangle and fill it in by rows until it looks like this:

```
      X X
   X  X X  X
   X  X X  X
   X  X X  X
      X X
```

4. Count the number of students inside of the rope boundary and compare this with the estimates made earlier.

☞ Once they have learned a movement with their bodies and have created a symbolic formula for that movement, often the formula alone can trigger the body knowing of the movement and, in turn, the meaning of the formula. This happens because the pattern has been encoded in the brain through the physical activity. An example of this can be seen when Olympic athletes use imagination exercises to improve the performance of their sport, or when children learn social roles through creative play.

5. Have students now return to their seats and with a partner create a symbolic formula that describes what they have just experienced: how many people it takes to fill in a rectangle that is four students wide by five students long.

6. Now have the entire class form itself into a circle. Have the class guess how many steps it will take to get around the outside of the circle.

7. Choose five different students to walk the circumference of the circle, one at a time, counting the number of steps they take. Record their numbers on the board or overhead.

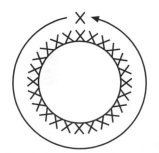

8. Ask the students if they have any ideas on other ways to figure out how many steps it takes to to get around the circle. Now have the same students walk the diameter of the circle, counting the number of steps they take. Again record the numbers.

9. Now ask the class to notice the relationship between the number of steps it takes to get around the circle compared to the number to get across it. What do you notice? Approximately how many times across would equal one time around?

10. Again have students return to their seats with a partner. Together they are to create a symbolic formula to explain what they have just experienced.

11. Now write the classical formulas for finding the area of a rectangle and for finding the circumference of a circle on the board and explain the formulas to the students: $A = l \times w$ and $C = \pi d$

☛ This comparison helps students bridge the formulas from the textbook into their own experience, for they have actually "embodied" the formulas!

12. Have student pairs compare the formula they wrote to the formula on the board. Listen carefully as they talk and help them understand the relationship between their formula and experience and the classical geometric formula for these things.

STAGE IV

☛ The goal of the transfer part of the lesson is to help students take what they have learned in the lesson and apply it in other areas of their schoolwork and in their everyday lives outside of school. The reflection on using the body to help learn information increases students' awareness of their own bodily/kinesthetic intelligence and how to make it work better for them.

TRANSFER

Reflect on the lesson with the students in the following manner:

1. Discuss what it was like to use the body to learn. Ask questions like the following:

   • Which of the two formulas was easiest to understand with your body? Why?

   • Which was most difficult? Why?

- How did using your body help you understand the formulas?
- What ideas do you have about other ways you could use your body to help you with your learning (in both mathematics and other subjects)?

2. Create columns for the rectangle and for the circle.

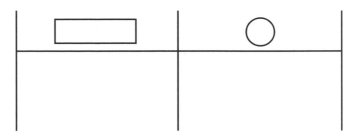

☛ This reflection on the formulas helps students see that they have gained something they can use in their lives outside of the classroom situation. Education research clearly shows that if the payoff of a lesson is immediate, the motivation for learning will dramatically increase.

Now brainstorm with the class when in their everyday lives these formulas might come in handy. Following are some examples:

- Will a 14" diameter pizza feed the number of people at your table? (How many inches of pizza will each get?)
- How many 2" x 3" photos would fit on an 8 ½" x 11" page?

SPIRAL ADAPTATIONS OF THE LESSON

Elementary School Level

1. Focus the lesson on learning to divide wholes into parts and on understanding the meaning of simple fractions.

2. Learn the meaning of one half, one third, and one fourth by tearing paper and then drawing pictures of the results; for example:

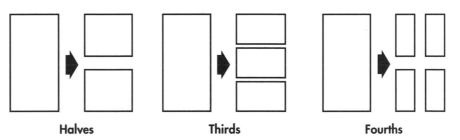

Halves　　　　**Thirds**　　　　**Fourths**

3. Have the students stand as a group, then divide themselves in half, into thirds, and then into fourths when you hold up signs with pictures like those above. Help them transfer these pictures to the fraction symbols that mean the same thing, namely:

$1/2$　　　　　　$1/3$　　　　　　$1/4$

Secondary School Level

1. Focus the lesson on learning the paper-and-pencil math process for finding unknown quantities in algebraic equations.

2. Practice "embodying" written math operations in physical movements. For example, physically demonstrate answers to various math problems such as

$$10 \div 5 = ? \quad \text{or} \quad \frac{(3+1)}{2} \times 2 = ?$$

3. Have students physically become different equations and find the unknown quantities with their bodies; for example,

$$\frac{(2 + x)}{2} = 4$$

4. Have them relate their discoveries to math operations they know can produce the same results.

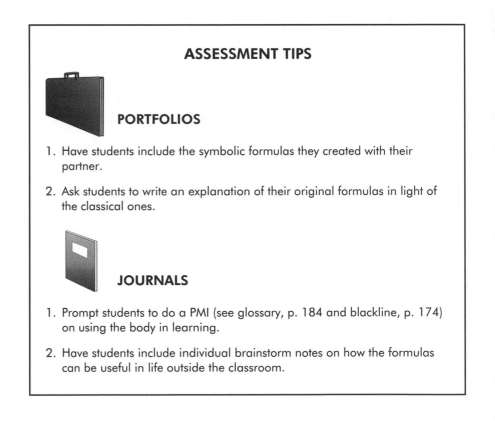

ASSESSMENT TIPS

PORTFOLIOS

1. Have students include the symbolic formulas they created with their partner.

2. Ask students to write an explanation of their original formulas in light of the classical ones.

JOURNALS

1. Prompt students to do a PMI (see glossary, p. 184 and blackline, p. 174) on using the body in learning.

2. Have students include individual brainstorm notes on how the formulas can be useful in life outside the classroom.

Look to the Past . . .

Rethink a lesson you have completed recently. How would you restructure it to teach *for* and *with* bodily/kinesthetic intelligence?

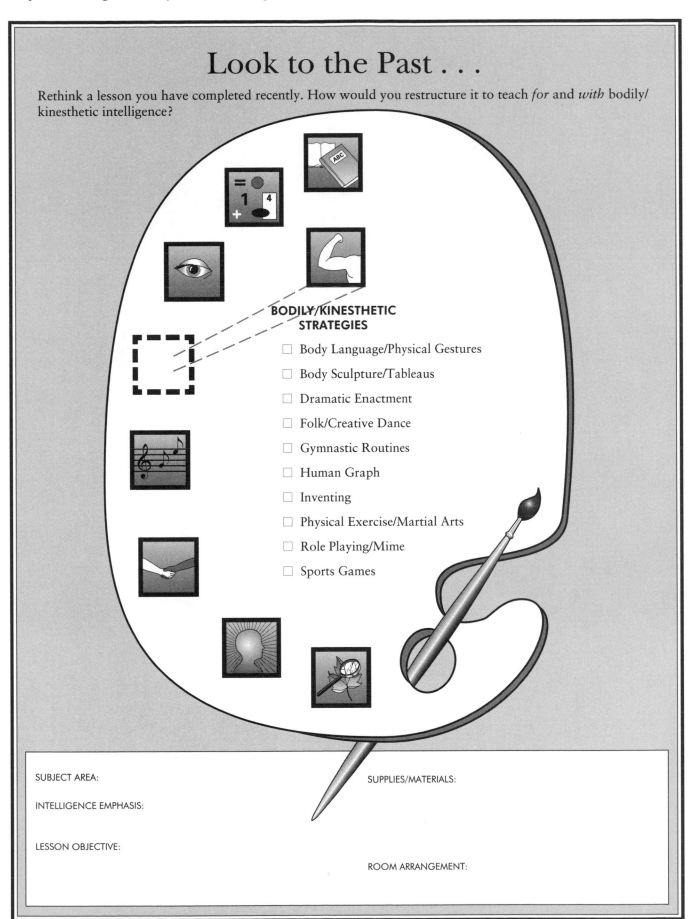

BODILY/KINESTHETIC STRATEGIES

- ☐ Body Language/Physical Gestures
- ☐ Body Sculpture/Tableaus
- ☐ Dramatic Enactment
- ☐ Folk/Creative Dance
- ☐ Gymnastic Routines
- ☐ Human Graph
- ☐ Inventing
- ☐ Physical Exercise/Martial Arts
- ☐ Role Playing/Mime
- ☐ Sports Games

SUBJECT AREA:

INTELLIGENCE EMPHASIS:

LESSON OBJECTIVE:

SUPPLIES/MATERIALS:

ROOM ARRANGEMENT:

Look to the Future . . .

Think about an upcoming lesson. How would you structure it to teach *for* and *with* bodily/kinesthetic intelligence?

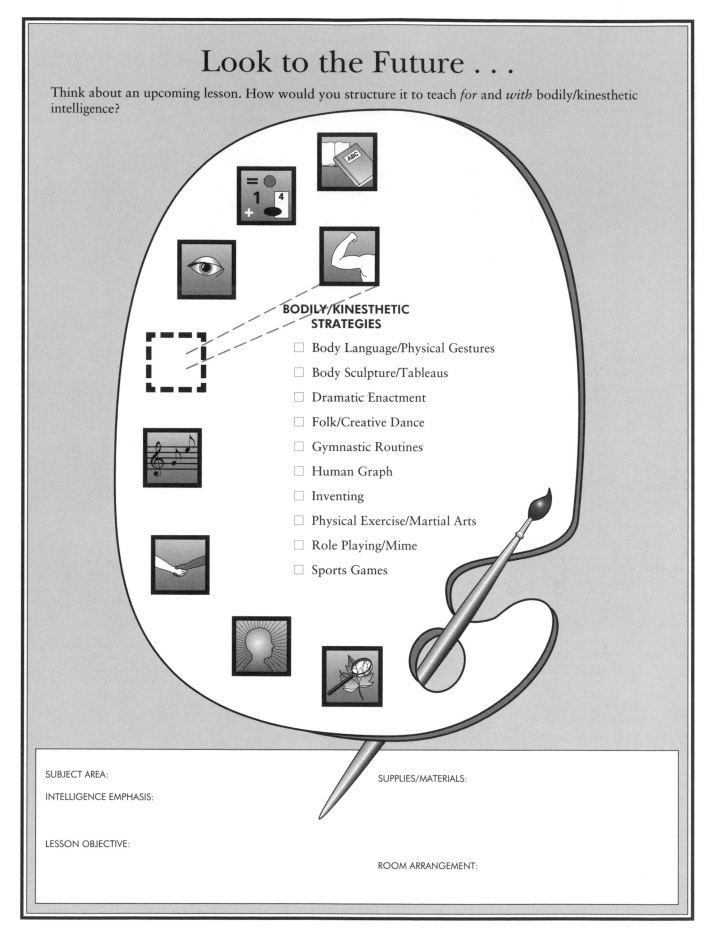

BODILY/KINESTHETIC STRATEGIES

- ☐ Body Language/Physical Gestures
- ☐ Body Sculpture/Tableaus
- ☐ Dramatic Enactment
- ☐ Folk/Creative Dance
- ☐ Gymnastic Routines
- ☐ Human Graph
- ☐ Inventing
- ☐ Physical Exercise/Martial Arts
- ☐ Role Playing/Mime
- ☐ Sports Games

SUBJECT AREA:

INTELLIGENCE EMPHASIS:

LESSON OBJECTIVE:

SUPPLIES/MATERIALS:

ROOM ARRANGEMENT:

LESSON PLANNING IDEAS
Bodily/Kinesthetic

HISTORY	MATHEMATICS	LANGUAGE ARTS	SCIENCE & HEALTH	GLOBAL STUDIES & GEOGRAPHY	FAMILY/CONSUMER SCIENCES, INDUSTRIAL TECHNOLOGY, & PE	FINE ARTS
Perform and/or create dramas from a period of history	Use different parts of the body to measure things	Play The Parts of a Sentence charades	Role-play the parts and dynamics of the life of a cell	Learn folk dances of a culture being studied	Learn and perfect various multitracking* routines	Create the dance equivalent for different inventions
Reenact great scenes or moments from history for today	Add and subtract members to and from a group to learn about fractions	"Embody" (act out) the meaning of vocabulary words	Create the rotation of planets with the class members acting as the solar system	Create gestures to represent the legend of a map	Invent something in shop class such as a new household tool	Create human sculpture tableau* to express an idea
Hold an historical period, costume, and food day	Design something that requires applying math concepts	Act out a story or play that you are studying	Become and act out the different states of matter	Play physical movement games from another culture	Practice physical movements in your mind then with your body	Make up gestures for parts of a musical score
Play Great Moments From the Past charades	Create and act out a play in which the characters are geometric shapes	Learn the alphabet by body movements and physical gestures	Conduct a series of hands-on scientific experiments	Simulate going shopping using currency from another country	Make up a new kind of snack food, prepare it, and eat it	Design a "live painting"* of a classical work
Learn dances from previous periods of history (e.g., minuet)	Make up a playground game that uses math concepts or operations	Make up a Parts of Speech folk dance	Study and try various biofeedback* techniques or methods	Study body language from different cultural situations	Create and perform a drama on how a computer operates	Practice doing impromptu dramatic mime activities

* See Glossary

SkyLight Training and Publishing Inc.

CHAPTER

5

TEACHING WITH MUSICAL/RHYTHMIC INTELLIGENCE

THE PAST IS ALIVE WITH THE SOUND OF MUSIC

A History Lesson:
Elementary School Level

Lesson Palette: *Musical/Rhythmic* Emphasis

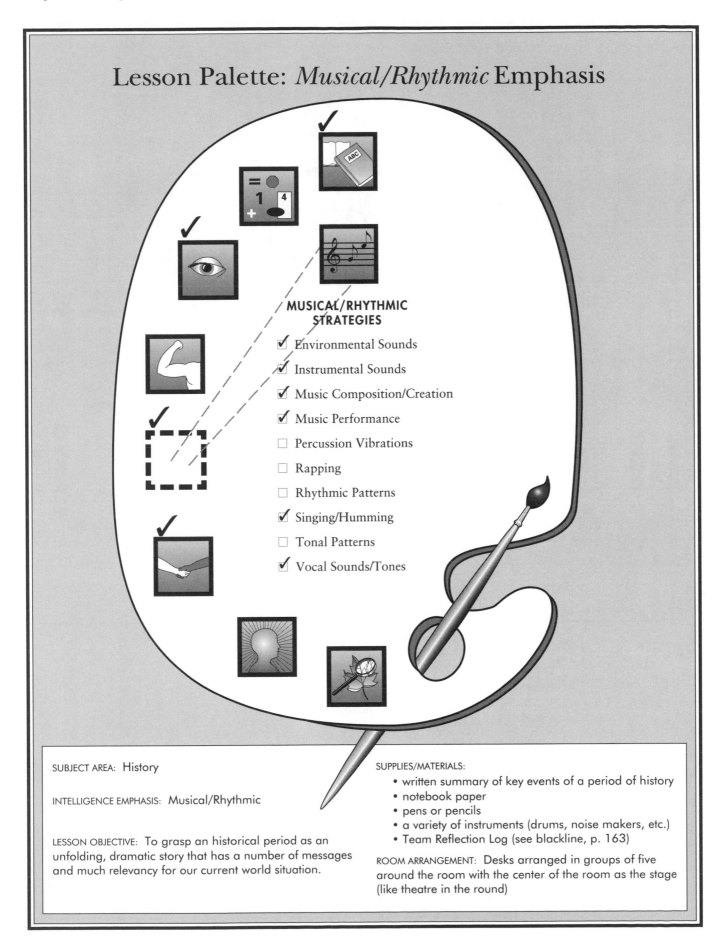

MUSICAL/RHYTHMIC STRATEGIES

☑ Environmental Sounds
☑ Instrumental Sounds
☑ Music Composition/Creation
☑ Music Performance
☐ Percussion Vibrations
☐ Rapping
☐ Rhythmic Patterns
☑ Singing/Humming
☐ Tonal Patterns
☑ Vocal Sounds/Tones

SUBJECT AREA: History

INTELLIGENCE EMPHASIS: Musical/Rhythmic

LESSON OBJECTIVE: To grasp an historical period as an unfolding, dramatic story that has a number of messages and much relevancy for our current world situation.

SUPPLIES/MATERIALS:
• written summary of key events of a period of history
• notebook paper
• pens or pencils
• a variety of instruments (drums, noise makers, etc.)
• Team Reflection Log (see blackline, p. 163)

ROOM ARRANGEMENT: Desks arranged in groups of five around the room with the center of the room as the stage (like theatre in the round)

THE LESSON . . .

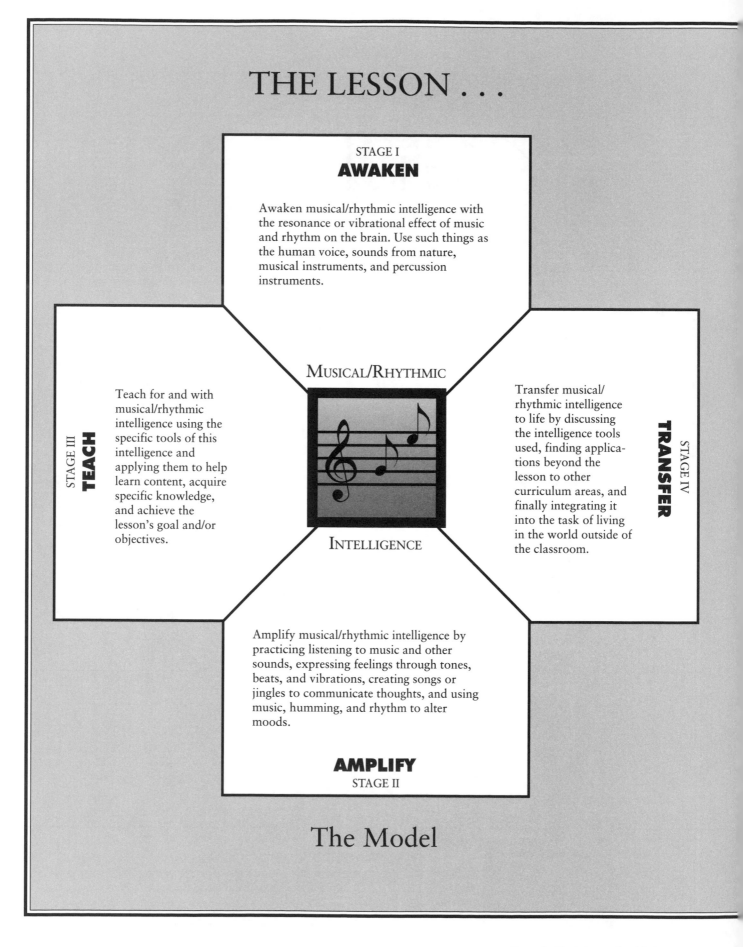

STAGE I
AWAKEN

Awaken musical/rhythmic intelligence with the resonance or vibrational effect of music and rhythm on the brain. Use such things as the human voice, sounds from nature, musical instruments, and percussion instruments.

MUSICAL/RHYTHMIC

INTELLIGENCE

STAGE III TEACH

Teach for and with musical/rhythmic intelligence using the specific tools of this intelligence and applying them to help learn content, acquire specific knowledge, and achieve the lesson's goal and/or objectives.

STAGE IV TRANSFER

Transfer musical/rhythmic intelligence to life by discussing the intelligence tools used, finding applications beyond the lesson to other curriculum areas, and finally integrating it into the task of living in the world outside of the classroom.

Amplify musical/rhythmic intelligence by practicing listening to music and other sounds, expressing feelings through tones, beats, and vibrations, creating songs or jingles to communicate thoughts, and using music, humming, and rhythm to alter moods.

AMPLIFY
STAGE II

The Model

SkyLight Training and Publishing Inc.

. . . AT A GLANCE

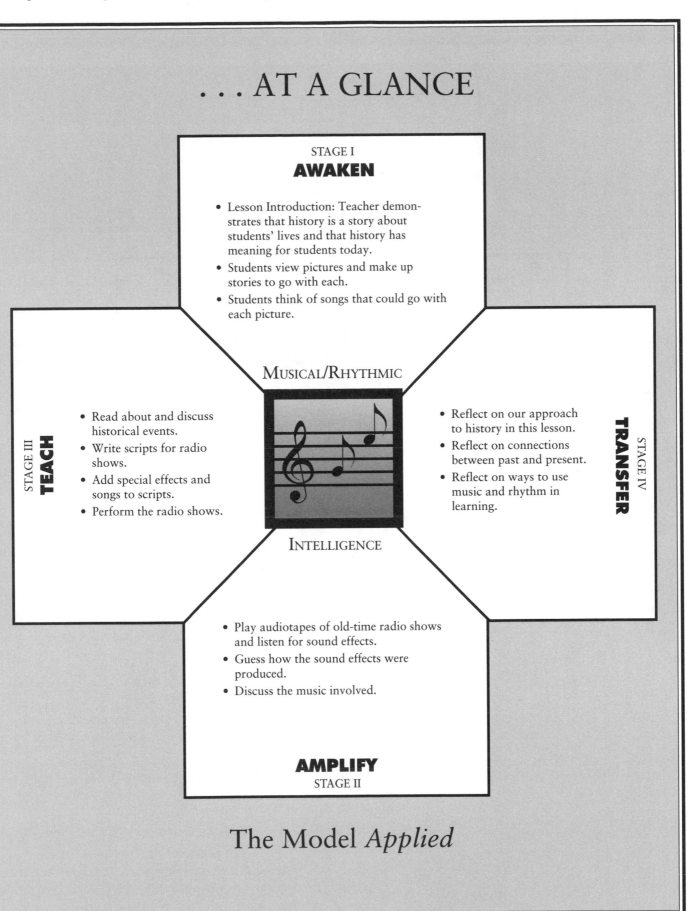

STAGE I
AWAKEN

- Lesson Introduction: Teacher demonstrates that history is a story about students' lives and that history has meaning for students today.
- Students view pictures and make up stories to go with each.
- Students think of songs that could go with each picture.

MUSICAL/RHYTHMIC

STAGE III
TEACH

- Read about and discuss historical events.
- Write scripts for radio shows.
- Add special effects and songs to scripts.
- Perform the radio shows.

STAGE IV
TRANSFER

- Reflect on our approach to history in this lesson.
- Reflect on connections between past and present.
- Reflect on ways to use music and rhythm in learning.

INTELLIGENCE

- Play audiotapes of old-time radio shows and listen for sound effects.
- Guess how the sound effects were produced.
- Discuss the music involved.

AMPLIFY
STAGE II

The Model *Applied*

SkyLight Training and Publishing Inc.

The Past Is Alive With
the Sound of Music

A History Lesson with

Musical/Rhythmic Intelligence

Lesson Procedures

INTRODUCTION

☞ In some ways the consciousness-altering effect of musical/rhythmic intelligence is greater than any of the other intelligences, precisely because of the impact of music on the state of the brain. Music, rhythm, and sound possess tremendous evocative power in our lives. Just think about how music and rhythm can calm you when you are stressed, stimulate you when you are bored, inspire your religious beliefs, national loyalty, or feelings for a beloved, and help you express experiences of great loss or intense joy. Also consider how effectively music is used in all forms of television and radio advertising! Both the left and right hemispheres of the brain are involved in musical/rhythmic intelligence. The left hemisphere is involved in the formal, systematic approach to music and rhythm. For example, we can learn to read notes, beat out a prescribed rhythm, and recognize different tones and/or instruments. The right hemisphere is the place of the sheer enjoyment of music for its own sake, whether or not we know anything about it as a formal system.

History is a story about our lives—where we have come from and where we are going. In this lesson students will illustrate an event from the past with sound, music, and rhythmic patterns. First, they will learn about something that happened in American history, either by reading a short article or by hearing a teacher lecture. Then, in cooperative groups, they will create songs and sound effects for retelling the story as if it were an old-time radio show. Tell the students that this lesson will emphasize the musical/rhythmic way of knowing. Ask them to be aware of this as they work on the lesson.

In addition to the musical/rhythmic emphasis of this lesson, verbal/linguistic, visual/spatial, and interpersonal intelligences are involved. Verbal/linguistic intelligence tools are employed at several points: reading, answering questions, and writing about an historical event. Interpersonal intelligence is involved in working with a team. Visual/spatial intelligence is accessed through using pictures, both in the opening exercise and in the pictures of historical scenes.

STAGE I

☞ Musical/rhythmic intelligence is activated by the resonance or vibrational effect of music, rhythm, and sound on the brain.

AWAKEN

1. Begin by showing students a series of pictures from a magazine. Ask volunteers to tell what they think is happening in the pictures. (Note: Try for a variety of pictures, such as people relaxing

As students make music and other sounds as the accompaniment for various pictures and stories, the effect of these sounds activates the musical centers of the brain (both left and right) and, with it, an immensely creative way of knowing.

Remember that the more sounds you can get the students to make, the greater will be the effect on the brain, because the vibrational impact on the brain catalyzes this way of knowing. As students are given permission to express themselves and their feelings through sound (beyond the traditional speaking of words), many of them will be opened to realms of knowing and understanding that transcend verbal expression.

on a beach, people involved in an argument, a family eating dinner, etc.)

2. Ask the class to imagine that these scenes are on television but something is wrong and they cannot see the pictures. Ask them how they could figure out what was happening. Make a list on the board or overhead of such things as the dialogue, the music being played, sounds effects, etc.

3. Now have them think of a kind of music that might be played for each picture which would help someone know what was happening. Prompt the class hum or sing it.

4. Ask them to think of sounds and noises that would be necessary to help someone know what was happening if they couldn't see the picture. Encourage the class again make some of the sounds.

STAGE II

☞ Enhancing musical/rhythmic intelligence has nothing to do with what is usually referred to as musical talent. It is rather knowing how to use music and rhythm to put ourselves into optimal states for dealing creatively with different situations. Likewise, we can learn to sense different moods, paces, themes, and ideas that are embedded in a piece of music or a rhythmic pattern which are inexpressible in words.

☞ In the listening, you are trying to draw them in to a new experience; namely, a world where there was no television. You help them catalyze their active imagination as they listen to the radio shows. By beginning with a short lecture you sensitize them to, and intrigue them with, the possibilities of communication by sound alone.

☞ By having students try to figure out what was done to actually produce the various background sounds, you are preparing them to come up with creative ideas for augmenting their own radio shows with sound and music in the next part of the lesson.

 **AMPLIFY**

1. Give a short lecture on the old days of radio, before television. Remind students that people only had radios, so when a radio story was being told the storytellers had to use special sounds, music, conversation between people, and different noises to help the listening audience understand the story. For example, they would often use wooden blocks to make it sound as if a horse were running, or they would rattle a bag of broken glass to make it sound as if a window had been broken.

2. Play several examples of different kinds of old radio shows so they get a sense of what this was like. (Note: You might try the *Lone Ranger, Fibber McGee and Molly, The Shadow* or some other suspense or detective show. Make sure the segments you play illustrate the importance of sound and music in these productions.)

3. Ask the students the following:

   • How do you think the radio programs produced the different sounds?

   • How did the music help the story?

STAGE III

 **TEACH**

1. Divide the students into cooperative groups with four members in each group. For a musical way to break into groups, have everyone pull a song out of a hat. Then have the students start humming their songs and find their groups by identifying the students who are humming their song. Assign the roles of reader, encourager, recorder, and group organizer.

2. Pass out pictures, one picture per team, that depict important events from the early days of American history (e.g., Columbus landing on the shores of the New World, the signing of the Declaration of Independence, Abraham Lincoln at Gettysburg, etc.) On the back of each picture have one or two paragraphs that explain what is happening in the picture along with two or three discussion questions (see p. 162 for an example).

☞ The discussion questions help the teams rehearse the basic information in the paragraphs about the pictures. By asking them to record their team's answers to the question you are promoting discussion and whole-team understanding of the picture and paragraph. At the same time this accesses verbal/linguistic intelligence capacities.

3. Assign teams to look at their pictures while the reader reads the paragraph on the back. After reading the paragraph, the group organizer is to ask the discussion questions while the recorder writes down the team's answers.

4. Ask the students to recall the radio shows they listened to earlier. Tell them they are to create a radio show about their pictures and the stories they tell. Each team will perform its program for the class just like the old-time radio shows.

5. In order to get ready for the show, each team will

☞ The script-writing assignment is also a comprehension exercise and further utilizes verbal/linguistic intelligence capacities. When students move into the task of creating a song and/or finding a musical piece that will set up and conclude the radio show and illustrating their script with sound, they have moved to the heart of musical/rhythmic intelligence. In these tasks you are helping them to move beyond mere head knowledge of their event to a gut-level emotional understanding of what is going on.

   a. Write a simple script that tells the story of the picture and involves all members of the team with a speaking part.

   b. Create a song about the event and/or find a piece of music to start off and end the show. They can either make up the music themselves or find recorded music to play, or a combination of both!

   c. Decide on at least five special sound effects to be used during the show to help the audience understand what is happening.

   (Note: You will have to monitor the groups very closely to make sure they do not get stuck. You may have to become more actively involved with some groups than others. Also, this project could extend over several days with teams working on one part of the assignment each day.)

☞ As students perform their radio shows for each other, they help their fellow students know and learn using musical/rhythmic intelligence. The fact that the performing team cannot be seen by their classmates further activates and calls to the fore the fullness of musical/rhythmic intelligence, both in the performing team and in the listening class!

6. When they are ready, have the teams perform their show from another room using an amplification system to transmit the program to the main classroom (if possible). If you cannot do this, have them perform their shows from behind a screen so they are hidden from view and must rely only on sound to communicate their story. If you can, tape-record each show so they can listen to it later.

☛ You may have to do some re-teaching and/or clarifying at this point. Have the team that presented the program help you with any teaching that is needed so the whole class understands the event.

STAGE IV

☛ The goal of the transfer part of the lesson is to help students take what they have learned in the lesson and apply it in other areas of their schoolwork and in their everyday lives outside of school.

☛ You are asking them to synthesize the key learnings and implications from the lesson in terms of its relevance for today. This is a key element in building bridges between the past, the present, and the future. And, after all, this is what makes history worth studying in the first place.

7. After each team has completed its show, thank them for their work and ask the class some questions to check their understanding of the event that was portrayed.

 **TRANSFER**

1. Ask the whole class to reflect on the radio programs:

   • What do you remember from these different radio programs?

   • What sounds are still ringing in your ears?

   • What lines of dialogue do you remember?

   • What music stands out for you?

2. Pass out the Team Reflection Log to each individual (see blackline, p. 163). Post the names of the different shows on the board or overhead and have the teams write them in the appropriate columns.

3. For each show have the teams discuss the following questions and have each individual write down thoughts from the team:

   • What was the story being told? Can you remember its parts?

   • How did it make you feel?

   • What are your questions about this event?

   • Why is this story important for us today?

SPIRAL ADAPTATIONS OF THE LESSON

Middle School Level

1. Practice turning relatively simple information—parts of speech, multiplication tables, states, and capitals—into songs or raps.

2. Have students read material from their history textbook, then retell the story in their own words, illustrating it with songs or raps.

3. After creating several songs about history, turn them into a Broadway-style musical.

Secondary School Level

1. Focus the lesson on learning about the mood, feel, and temperament of a part of history through music, rhythm, and sound.

2. Learn to recognize patterns in music and rhythm that communicate such things as emotions, actions, and moods, as well as patterns that can evoke certain feelings in people.

3. Gather a series of examples of music from a period of history you have been studying (e.g., Gregorian chant, madrigal, minuet, waltz, cantata, etc.). Listen to the music and challenge students to describe what this period must have been like based on its music. Then discuss what today's music says about us! Compare students' impressions with textbook descriptions.

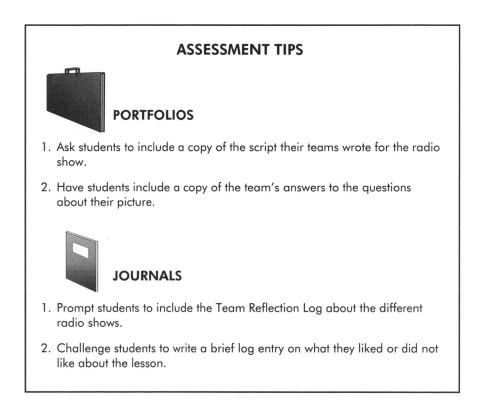

ASSESSMENT TIPS

PORTFOLIOS

1. Ask students to include a copy of the script their teams wrote for the radio show.

2. Have students include a copy of the team's answers to the questions about their picture.

JOURNALS

1. Prompt students to include the Team Reflection Log about the different radio shows.

2. Challenge students to write a brief log entry on what they liked or did not like about the lesson.

Look to the Past . . .

Rethink a lesson you have completed recently. How would you restructure it to teach *for* and *with* musical/rhythmic intelligence?

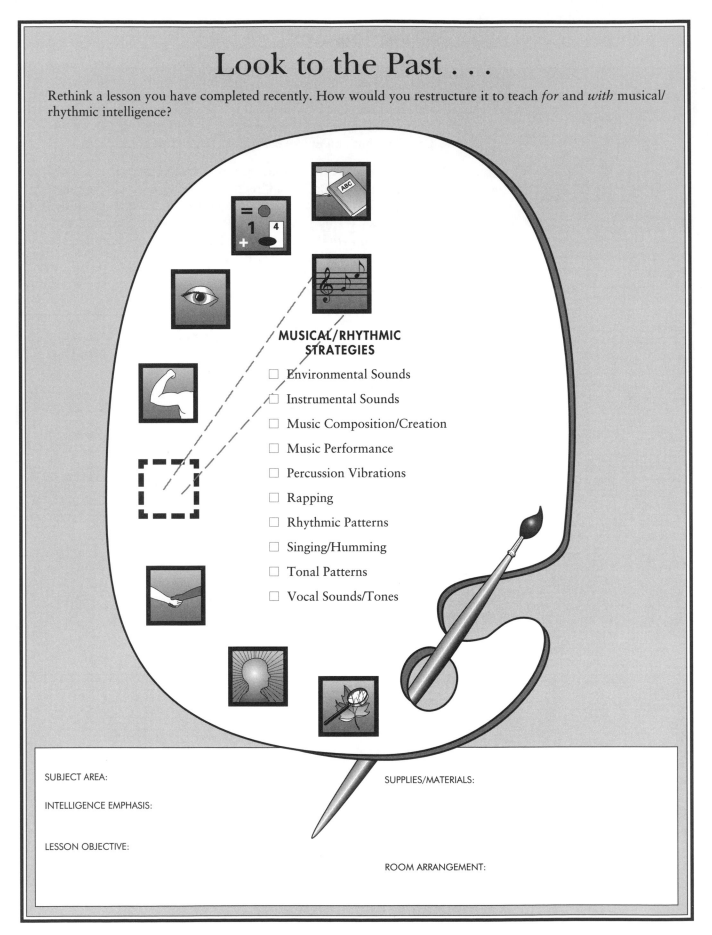

MUSICAL/RHYTHMIC STRATEGIES

- ☐ Environmental Sounds
- ☐ Instrumental Sounds
- ☐ Music Composition/Creation
- ☐ Music Performance
- ☐ Percussion Vibrations
- ☐ Rapping
- ☐ Rhythmic Patterns
- ☐ Singing/Humming
- ☐ Tonal Patterns
- ☐ Vocal Sounds/Tones

SUBJECT AREA:

INTELLIGENCE EMPHASIS:

LESSON OBJECTIVE:

SUPPLIES/MATERIALS:

ROOM ARRANGEMENT:

Look to the Future . . .

Think about a lesson you have coming up in the near future. How would you structure it to teach *for* and *with* musical/rhythmic intelligence?

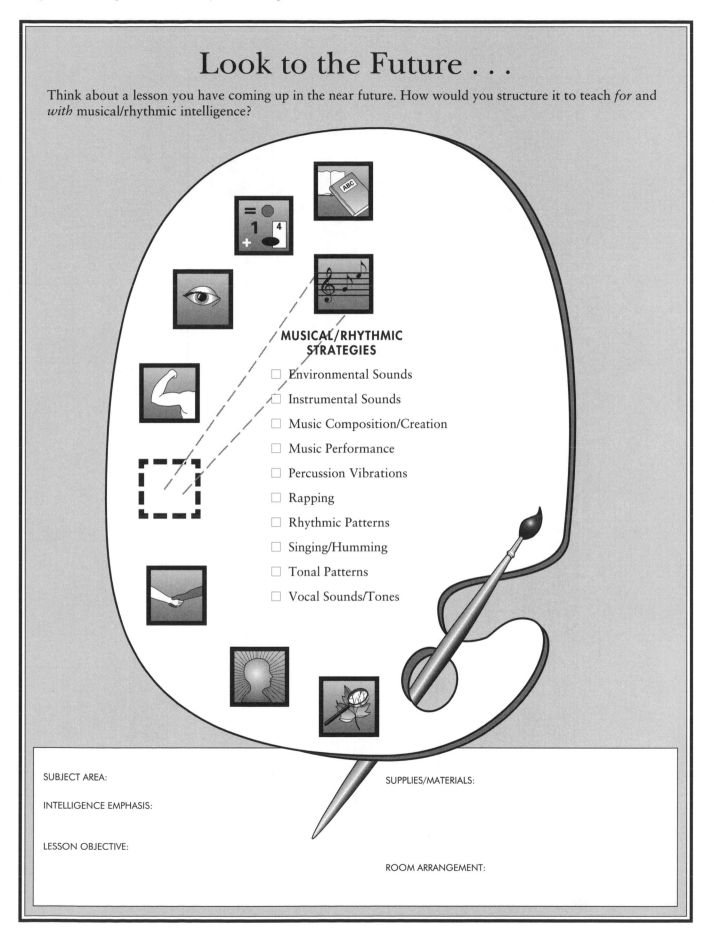

MUSICAL/RHYTHMIC STRATEGIES

- ☐ Environmental Sounds
- ☐ Instrumental Sounds
- ☐ Music Composition/Creation
- ☐ Music Performance
- ☐ Percussion Vibrations
- ☐ Rapping
- ☐ Rhythmic Patterns
- ☐ Singing/Humming
- ☐ Tonal Patterns
- ☐ Vocal Sounds/Tones

SUBJECT AREA:

INTELLIGENCE EMPHASIS:

LESSON OBJECTIVE:

SUPPLIES/MATERIALS:

ROOM ARRANGEMENT:

LESSON PLANNING IDEAS
Musical/Rhythmic

HISTORY	MATHEMATICS	LANGUAGE ARTS	SCIENCE & HEALTH	GLOBAL STUDIES & GEOGRAPHY	FAMILY/CONSUMER SCIENCES, INDUSTRIAL TECHNOLOGY, & PE	FINE ARTS
Analyze different historical periods through their music	Learn mathematical operations through songs and jingles	Learn Morse Code and practice communicating with it	Learn to use music to reduce stress	Listen to music from different cultures	Perform physical exercise routines in sync with music	Play Guess the Rhythm or Guess the Instrument with musical pieces
Create a series of key dates in history raps	Learn addition and subtraction through drum beats	Use different kinds of music for different kinds of writing	Listen to sounds of things in the natural world	Play musical instruments from around the world	Learn to recognize shop machines through their sounds	Draw or paint a piece of music as it plays
Make musical instruments from the past and compose a piece	Play a rhythm game* to learn multiplication tables	Learn and practice phonetic punctuation (a lá Victor Borge)	Experiment with the effect of vibration on sand in a metal plate	Create a sound- or tonal-based legend for a map	Record and recognize the varying sounds of a computer operating	Turn a nonmusical play into a musical
Teach songs that were sung in previous eras (e.g., Gregorian chant)	Break a set of tones into various groups to learn division tables	Create songs or raps to teach grammar and syntax	Try various humming patterns to see how they change mood	Learn characteristic rhythm patterns of different cultures	Experiment with the effect of different kinds of music on how you eat	Practice impromptu music composition
Watch films about the past and focus on the sounds of history	Make up sounds for different math operations and processes	Illustrate a story or poem with appropriate sounds	Assign sounds to systems you are studying such as the nervous system or circulatory system	Sing songs from nations or countries being studied	Use music to help improve keyboarding skills and speed	Make up a creative or interpretive dance to a piece of music

* See Glossary

TEACHING WITH
INTERPERSONAL
INTELLIGENCE

FORMING A PERSONAL
ADVISORY COUNCIL

A Literature Lesson:
Middle School Level

Lesson Palette: *Interpersonal* Emphasis

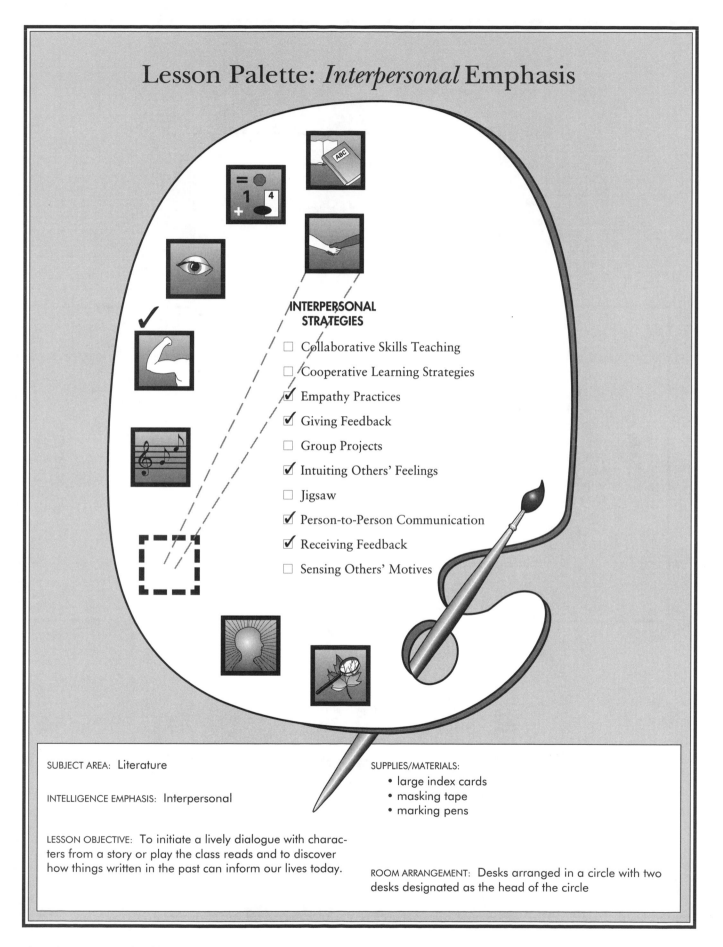

INTERPERSONAL STRATEGIES

- ☐ Collaborative Skills Teaching
- ☐ Cooperative Learning Strategies
- ☑ Empathy Practices
- ☑ Giving Feedback
- ☐ Group Projects
- ☑ Intuiting Others' Feelings
- ☐ Jigsaw
- ☑ Person-to-Person Communication
- ☑ Receiving Feedback
- ☐ Sensing Others' Motives

SUBJECT AREA: Literature

INTELLIGENCE EMPHASIS: Interpersonal

LESSON OBJECTIVE: To initiate a lively dialogue with characters from a story or play the class reads and to discover how things written in the past can inform our lives today.

SUPPLIES/MATERIALS:
- large index cards
- masking tape
- marking pens

ROOM ARRANGEMENT: Desks arranged in a circle with two desks designated as the head of the circle

THE LESSON . . .

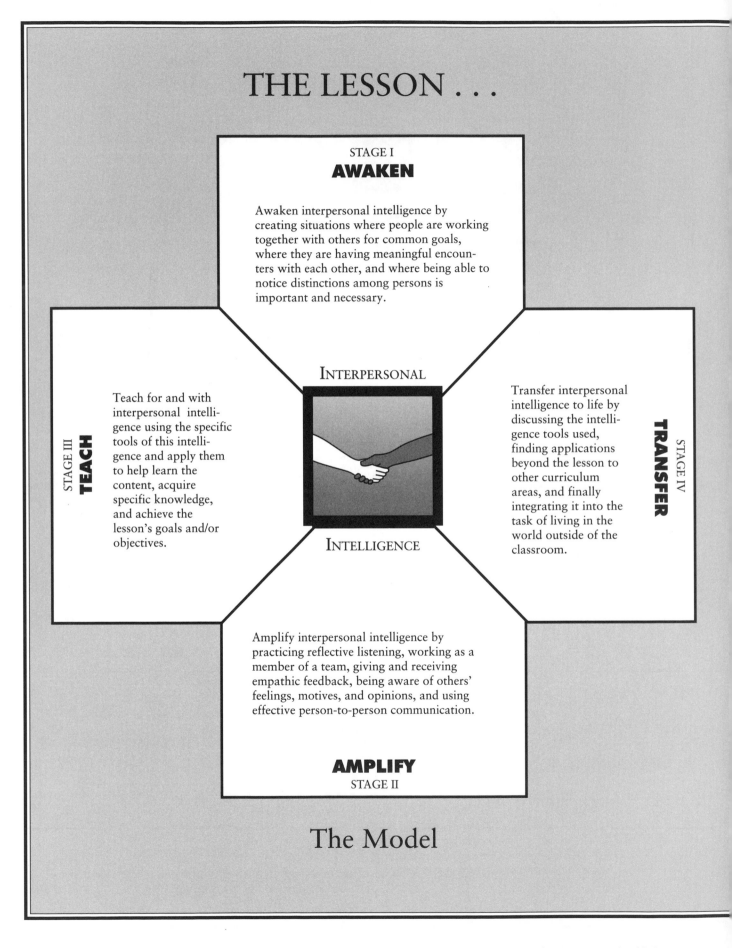

STAGE I
AWAKEN

Awaken interpersonal intelligence by creating situations where people are working together with others for common goals, where they are having meaningful encounters with each other, and where being able to notice distinctions among persons is important and necessary.

INTERPERSONAL

STAGE III
TEACH

Teach for and with interpersonal intelligence using the specific tools of this intelligence and apply them to help learn the content, acquire specific knowledge, and achieve the lesson's goals and/or objectives.

Transfer interpersonal intelligence to life by discussing the intelligence tools used, finding applications beyond the lesson to other curriculum areas, and finally integrating it into the task of living in the world outside of the classroom.

STAGE IV
TRANSFER

INTELLIGENCE

Amplify interpersonal intelligence by practicing reflective listening, working as a member of a team, giving and receiving empathic feedback, being aware of others' feelings, motives, and opinions, and using effective person-to-person communication.

AMPLIFY
STAGE II

The Model

SkyLight Training and Publishing Inc.

. . . AT A GLANCE

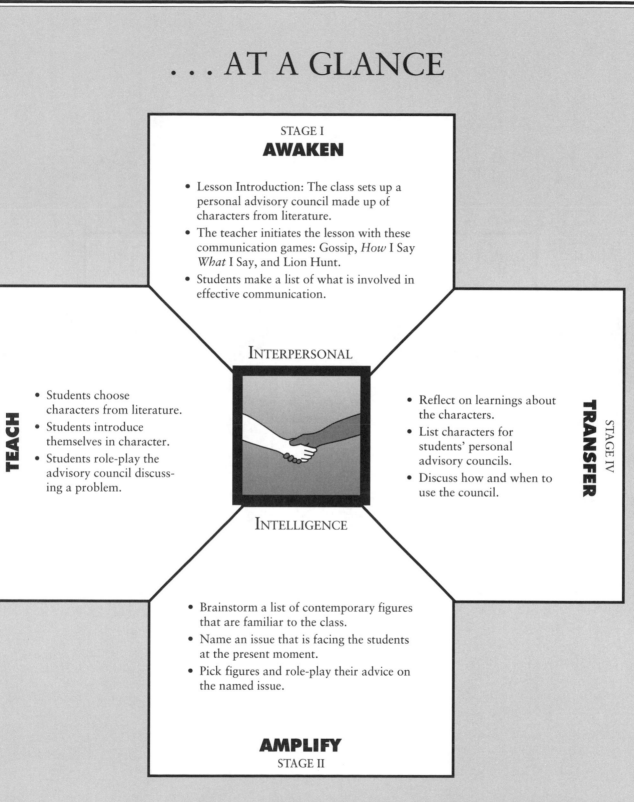

STAGE I
AWAKEN

- Lesson Introduction: The class sets up a personal advisory council made up of characters from literature.
- The teacher initiates the lesson with these communication games: Gossip, *How* I Say *What* I Say, and Lion Hunt.
- Students make a list of what is involved in effective communication.

INTERPERSONAL

STAGE III
TEACH

- Students choose characters from literature.
- Students introduce themselves in character.
- Students role-play the advisory council discussing a problem.

STAGE IV
TRANSFER

- Reflect on learnings about the characters.
- List characters for students' personal advisory councils.
- Discuss how and when to use the council.

INTELLIGENCE

- Brainstorm a list of contemporary figures that are familiar to the class.
- Name an issue that is facing the students at the present moment.
- Pick figures and role-play their advice on the named issue.

AMPLIFY
STAGE II

The Model *Applied*

Forming a Personal
Advisory Council

A LITERATURE LESSON WITH

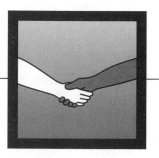

Interpersonal Intelligence

Lesson Procedures

☛ Interpersonal intelligence is the person-to-person way of knowing, and as such, it must rely on all the other intelligences in order to express itself. It therefore involves a great deal of neurological activity including both the right and left hemispheres of the brain, the limbic system (the seat of emotion), the cortex (the place of relating, loyalty, and trust), and the neocortex (the complex, eighth-inch thick covering of the brain which is responsible for higher-order thinking and reasoning processes). In addition, researchers have observed that the frontal lobes of the brain are active in interpersonal encounters, although not much beyond this is known about their function. (See fig. 0.5, p.12).

INTRODUCTION

Literature is the study of other people's ideas and feelings about living. At the same time, to study literature is to study oneself—one's own ideas and feelings. In this lesson, students enter into dialogue with various characters from a story or play. In the process they will discover how things written in the past can inform their lives today. They will learn how to seek advice on contemporary problems and issues by consulting wisdom from the past. Inform the students that they will be using their interpersonal intelligence in this lesson and ask them to pay attention to what this is like and what happens as they use this way of knowing.

At least three ways of knowing beyond the interpersonal are active in this lesson. Verbal/linguistic intelligence is involved when students spontaneously create dialogue for a character from literature. Visual/spatial and bodily/kinesthetic intelligences are involved as they role-play a chosen character.

STAGE I

☛ The heartbeat of interpersonal intelligence is the sense of positive interdependence—we sink or swim together, two heads are better than one, and all of us can do more together than any one of us can do alone. It is awakened in situations that require the support,

AWAKEN

1. Begin by leading students in several communication/listening games. You might try such things as

   a. **The Gossip Game.** Whisper a message in one student's ear and have each in turn repeat the message by whispering it in their neighbor's ear until it has made its way around the class.

energy, and cooperation of other people to complete a given task. These communication games are designed to trigger both the desire to relate to each other and the use of some of the capacities that are part of interpersonal intelligence, especially the ability to listen to each other. When you ask students to list things that are involved in effective communication, you are creating an awareness that there are social skills that can be learned, and, like any skill, practiced and improved. Students are often deeply fascinated with this whole area of interpersonal relationships and the possibility of improving them. This is especially true for middle school and secondary students whose own peer relationships may be their most important locus of self-identity, esteem, and security. Almost any initiating activity that asks students to relate to and rely on each other will work to awaken this very powerful way of knowing.

Have the last student repeat the message aloud and note how it has changed in the process.

b. *How* I Say *What* I Say. Choose a short love poem and read it to the class. Then read it as if you are very upset. Have several students practice reading it in different ways and notice what happens to the message of the poem when it is read in different ways. For example, read the poem as if it were a comedy script, as if you were speaking to an infant, or as if you were totally bored.

c. **Lion Hunt.** Begin by saying (and have the class say with you), "We're going on a lion hunt, through the deepest jungle, we're going on a lion hunt and I'm going to take a _____." Fill in the blank with some item you think will be needed on the lion hunt. Then begin the chant again only this time when you get to the blank, ask the student sitting to your left to repeat what you said and add something of his or her own. The game proceeds around the circle with each student repeating all the previous items before adding their own.

2. On the board or overhead, have students brainstorm what is involved in effective communication and listening—Just what does it take?

3. Tell the class that in this lesson they are going to have a chance to communicate with and listen to characters from literature.

STAGE II

☛ This exercise requires the students to step outside of their own ideas, opinions, and feelings and to assume those of other people.

A certain degree of self-transcendence occurs here. As a result, students have an opportunity to unlearn some of the poor interpersonal habits they may have developed. Common among these habits are thinking there is only one right answer to a problem or issue, not being able to communicate effectively when there is disagreement, and getting so caught up in their own opinions, thoughts, and feelings that they completely miss what another person is trying to communicate.

 **AMPLIFY**

1. Tell the class that you want them to experiment with what it is like to stand in someone else's shoes and become another person.

2. Model the following process for the students and then let them practice with each other:

a. Brainstorm a list of contemporary figures that are familiar to the class.

b. Have students list five issues that are of concern to them at the present moment.

c. Pick a figure and one of the issues from the list and pretend that you are that person giving your advice or opinion about the issue. Speak in character as fully as you can.

d. Ask students to think of other things the figure might say or do in relation to the issue.

3. Ask for several volunteers to choose a different figure from the brainstorm list and to role-play their figure's advice, response, and opinions about another issue on the list.

4. Explain to students that they will do the same thing with characters from literature in the lesson.

SkyLight Training and Publishing Inc.

 **TEACH**

STAGE III

☛ The advisory council game provides an opportunity for students to use a wide range of their interpersonal knowing capacities to learn more about literature and to discover some of the wisdom of the past that can help them with their lives today.

Students should choose a character with whom they are familiar and with whom they already have a certain degree of identification. If more than one student has chosen a particular character, you may want them to sit together as a group, or you may want them to choose certain times or periods of the character's life to represent. In the choosing process they begin to establish an interpersonal linkage with their character. They then present themselves to the rest of the class in character. This presentation adds two other intelligences—visual/spatial when students actively imagine themselves as their character and bodily/kinesthetic when students make gestures or physical movements like the character would.

By having to become another person and give advice they imagine this person would give, students gain both a deeper appreciation of their character and a sense of personal connection to the past.

☛ By posing a modern-day problem to the advisory council you are helping students to integrate their knowledge about their character (and the story or play they represent) with their own lives. In this process students experience the fact that there are usually multiple perspectives on a given problem. Try to encourage the council members to occasionally talk among themselves, challenging each other, disagreeing, and arguing. However, do not let them get off on tangents and lose the focus of the discussion.

1. Pass out a large index card and marker to each student. Individually, they are to think of a character they have studied in literature whom they feel they know fairly well and can identify with in some way. (Note: You may have to prime the pump by reminding them of some of the stories or plays you have studied and help them think of some of the characters they have encountered.)

2. When they have chosen their characters, have them write the character's name on the index card so that everyone else can see. Distribute tape and instruct them to tape the name of their character to their chest. (Or, have them fold their card so it stands up on the desk in front of them.)

3. Now give them a moment to figure out how to introduce themselves in character to the rest of the class (e.g., My name is Pip, and I am filled with many great expectations for the future.) When they are ready, proceed around the circle with each student introducing him- or herself in character.

4. Explain that students will play a game in which they pretend that this group of characters is an advisory council trying to help someone solve a problem. Ask for a volunteer to be the advisee in the game.

5. Have the advisee name a real problem or issue that he or she is facing now that he or she would be willing to share with the class. Have him or her briefly tell the class what the issue is.

6. Now have the advisee ask the advisory council questions that relate to the issue or problem on which they need counsel. The advisee addresses the character by the name on the card, and the student behind the card responds as if they were their chosen character. (Note: Play the role of the moderator in this discussion, making sure that the students take turns and that all have a chance to participate. Keep it lively, and encourage the characters of the council to talk or argue with each other about the advice they are giving. The key is to help students stay in character as they speak.)

7. Conclude by going around the circle again with each member of the council having a chance to say a final word to the advisee. Then have the advisee tell the council what advice was helpful. Have everyone shake hands with each other and say, "It was good to see you again," etc.

8. Bring the game to a close by having students take off the character cards, come out of character, and talk about the process.

STAGE IV

☞ The goal of the transfer part of the lesson is to help students take what they have learned in the lesson and apply it to other areas of their schoolwork and their everyday lives outside of school.

   There are two dynamics of transfer that occur at this point: (1) students speak about what they learned about their character and/or the story or play in which the character appears, thus appropriating the content of the lesson; and (2) they list characters from literature they think could help them gain fresh perspectives on their own lives. They think about the possibility for further experimentation with the advisory council, thus making connections between the lesson and life beyond the classroom.

TRANSFER

1. Ask the class the following questions as a way to process the game:

   • What words of advice or comments do you remember?

   • What did you like about the exercise? dislike?

   • What was easy about the exercise? difficult?

2. Have students brainstorm a list of people they would like to have on their own personal advisory council and explain why they would choose them.

3. Ask students to individually write down situations in which they would use their council. What would be the most effective use of the council?

SPIRAL ADAPTATIONS OF THE LESSON

Elementary School Level

1. Focus the lesson on understanding characters from a story students have just read. What kind of characters are they? What do they like? How do they feel? Do you like them? Why or why not?

2. Practice role-playing conversations between different characters in the context of the story. Extend the story and see how characters relate and react in new situations.

3. Pretend the story characters are present in our world today. Role-play what it might be like if certain characters were the teacher of this class, what they would be like as a member of the family, and what it would be like if they were the student's best friend.

Secondary School Level

1. Focus the lesson on analyzing different characters and what they bring to the story or play. For example, they may represent certain motifs, different virtues (such as in a morality play), or various factors of the human condition (such as in a Shakespearean play).

2. Teach students how to create mind maps (see glossary, p. 182) that show all the different aspects of a character that they can think of.

3. Create a mock UN Security Council meeting with students playing the council members as if they were one of the characters they mind-mapped. Discuss such things as how to improve the plight of third-world countries, how to deal with an aggressor nation that violates the sovereignty of another, or how to protect the world's natural resources.

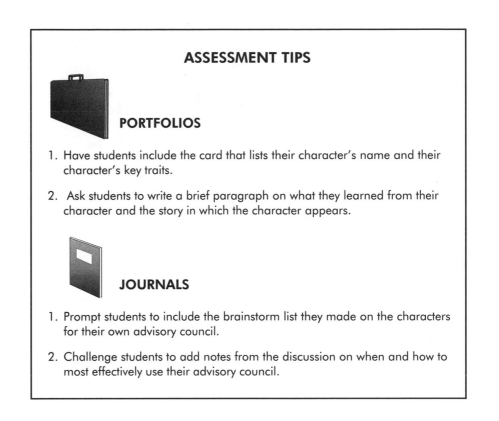

ASSESSMENT TIPS

PORTFOLIOS

1. Have students include the card that lists their character's name and their character's key traits.

2. Ask students to write a brief paragraph on what they learned from their character and the story in which the character appears.

JOURNALS

1. Prompt students to include the brainstorm list they made on the characters for their own advisory council.

2. Challenge students to add notes from the discussion on when and how to most effectively use their advisory council.

Look to the Past . . .

Rethink a lesson you have completed recently. How would you restructure it to teach *for* and *with* interpersonal intelligence?)

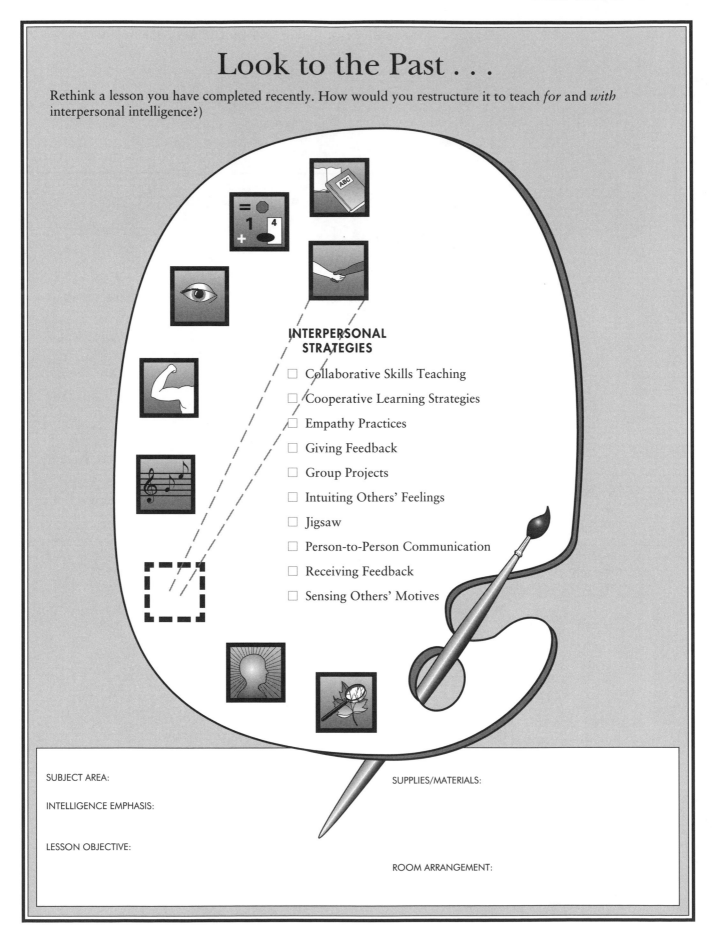

INTERPERSONAL STRATEGIES

- ☐ Collaborative Skills Teaching
- ☐ Cooperative Learning Strategies
- ☐ Empathy Practices
- ☐ Giving Feedback
- ☐ Group Projects
- ☐ Intuiting Others' Feelings
- ☐ Jigsaw
- ☐ Person-to-Person Communication
- ☐ Receiving Feedback
- ☐ Sensing Others' Motives

SUBJECT AREA:

INTELLIGENCE EMPHASIS:

LESSON OBJECTIVE:

SUPPLIES/MATERIALS:

ROOM ARRANGEMENT:

Look to the Future . . .

Think about a lesson you have coming up in the near future. How would you structure it to teach *for* and *with* interpersonal intelligence?

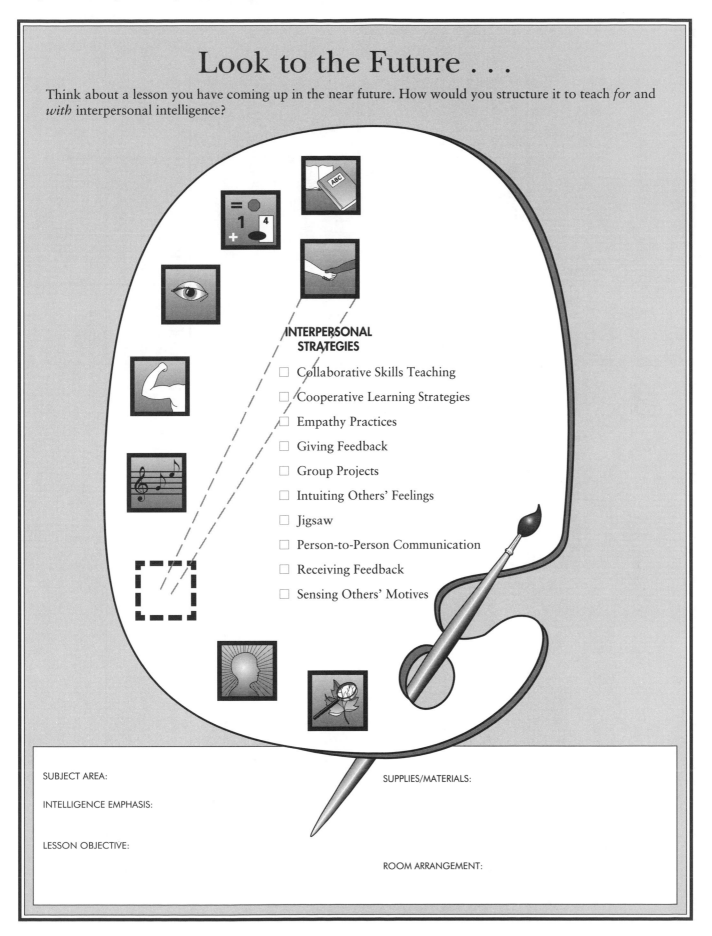

INTERPERSONAL STRATEGIES

- ☐ Collaborative Skills Teaching
- ☐ Cooperative Learning Strategies
- ☐ Empathy Practices
- ☐ Giving Feedback
- ☐ Group Projects
- ☐ Intuiting Others' Feelings
- ☐ Jigsaw
- ☐ Person-to-Person Communication
- ☐ Receiving Feedback
- ☐ Sensing Others' Motives

SUBJECT AREA:

INTELLIGENCE EMPHASIS:

LESSON OBJECTIVE:

SUPPLIES/MATERIALS:

ROOM ARRANGEMENT:

Lesson Planning Ideas
Interpersonal

HISTORY	MATHEMATICS	LANGUAGE ARTS	SCIENCE & HEALTH	GLOBAL STUDIES & GEOGRAPHY	FAMILY/CONSUMER SCIENCES, INDUSTRIAL TECHNOLOGY, & PE	FINE ARTS
Do an historical period investigation jigsaw**	Solve complex story problems in a group	Experiment with joint story writing—one starts then passes it on	Discuss Saying No to Drugs and create Say No strategies	Assume the perspective of another culture and discuss a news item	Teach and play a series of noncompetitive games*	Learn a new dance and teach it to others
Role-play a conversation with an important historical figure	Do a statistical research project and calculate percentages	Analyze a story and describe its message—reach a consensus	Assign group research projects—groups design and implement plans	Find the relation of geography or climate to cultural values and customs	Assign teams to prepare and serve meals from foreign countries	Create a team cooperative sculpture from clay
Pass over* into the lives of historical people and describe their feelings or thoughts	Each One Teach One* new math processes or operations	Use a human graph* to see where a group stands on an issue	Use lab teams for science experiments and exercises	Create scenarios of culture shock and analyze it for its causes	Use peer coaching teams* for individual shop projects	Sketch your partner with different expressions
Make a case for different perspectives on the Revolutionary War	Describe *everything* you do to solve a problem with a partner	Read poetry from different perspectives and in different moods	Discuss controversial health topics and write team position papers	Brainstorm and prioritize ways to overcome "ugly Americanism"*	Have students work in pairs to learn and improve sports skills	Practice Stop the Action and Improvise* with a play
Discuss the impact of key historical decisions on today's world	Have teams construct problems linking many math operations, then solve them	Conduct language drill exercises with a partner	Describe the before and after of key scientific paradigm shifts	Learn to read different kinds of maps, then teach someone how to understand them	Create cooperative computing teams to learn computer skills	Learn to sing rounds and countermelody* songs

* See Glossary
** See Glossary and Appendix C

SkyLight Training and Publishing Inc.

CHAPTER

7

TEACHING WITH INTRAPERSONAL INTELLIGENCE

HOW AM I INVOLVED AND WHAT CAN I DO?

A Current Events Lesson:
Secondary School Level

Lesson Palette: *Intrapersonal* Emphasis

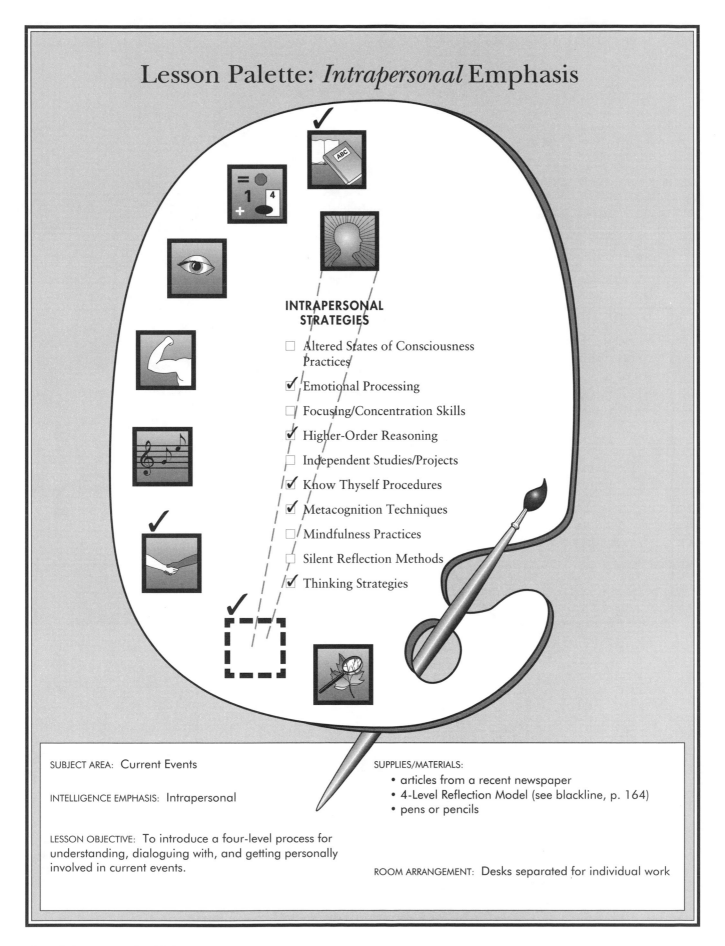

INTRAPERSONAL STRATEGIES

- ☐ Altered States of Consciousness Practices
- ☑ Emotional Processing
- ☐ Focusing/Concentration Skills
- ☑ Higher-Order Reasoning
- ☐ Independent Studies/Projects
- ☑ Know Thyself Procedures
- ☑ Metacognition Techniques
- ☐ Mindfulness Practices
- ☐ Silent Reflection Methods
- ☑ Thinking Strategies

SUBJECT AREA: Current Events

INTELLIGENCE EMPHASIS: Intrapersonal

LESSON OBJECTIVE: To introduce a four-level process for understanding, dialoguing with, and getting personally involved in current events.

SUPPLIES/MATERIALS:
- articles from a recent newspaper
- 4-Level Reflection Model (see blackline, p. 164)
- pens or pencils

ROOM ARRANGEMENT: Desks separated for individual work

THE LESSON . . .

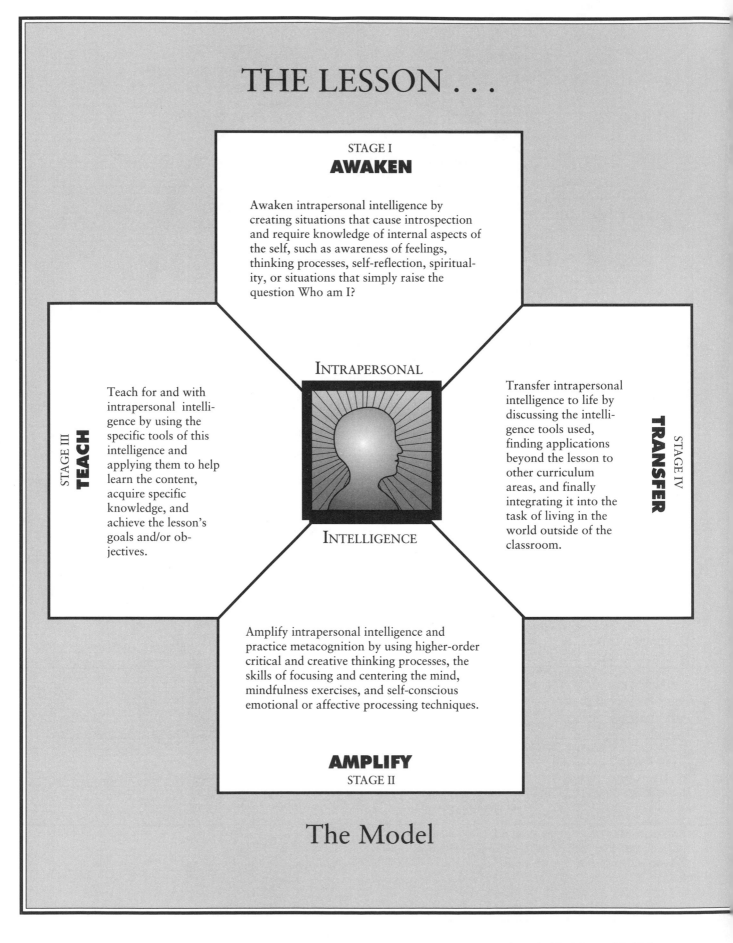

STAGE I
AWAKEN

Awaken intrapersonal intelligence by creating situations that cause introspection and require knowledge of internal aspects of the self, such as awareness of feelings, thinking processes, self-reflection, spirituality, or situations that simply raise the question Who am I?

INTRAPERSONAL

STAGE III
TEACH

Teach for and with intrapersonal intelligence by using the specific tools of this intelligence and applying them to help learn the content, acquire specific knowledge, and achieve the lesson's goals and/or objectives.

INTELLIGENCE

Transfer intrapersonal intelligence to life by discussing the intelligence tools used, finding applications beyond the lesson to other curriculum areas, and finally integrating it into the task of living in the world outside of the classroom.

STAGE IV
TRANSFER

Amplify intrapersonal intelligence and practice metacognition by using higher-order critical and creative thinking processes, the skills of focusing and centering the mind, mindfulness exercises, and self-conscious emotional or affective processing techniques.

AMPLIFY
STAGE II

The Model

SkyLight Training and Publishing Inc.

. . . AT A GLANCE

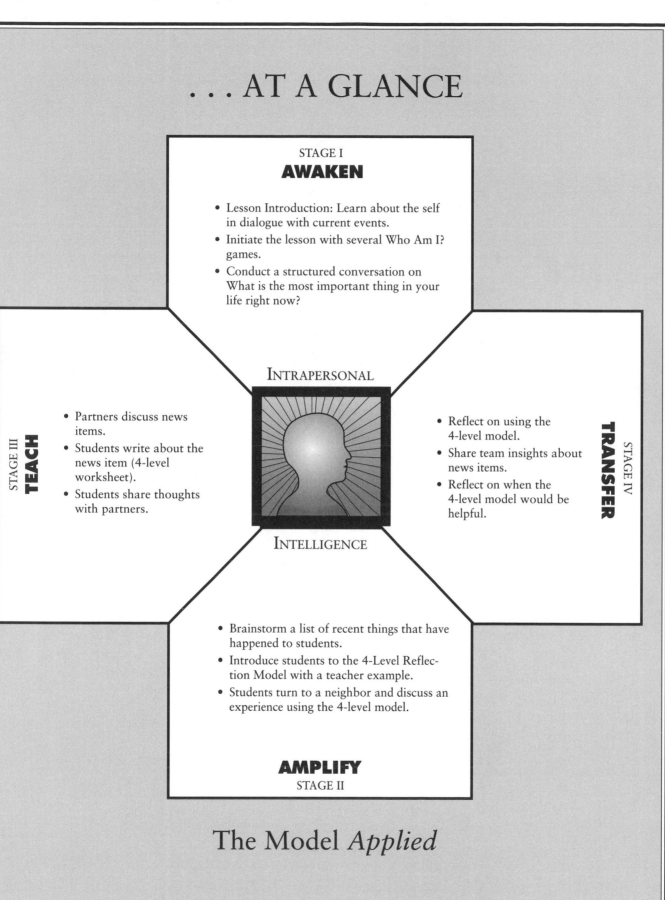

STAGE I
AWAKEN

- Lesson Introduction: Learn about the self in dialogue with current events.
- Initiate the lesson with several Who Am I? games.
- Conduct a structured conversation on What is the most important thing in your life right now?

STAGE III
TEACH

- Partners discuss news items.
- Students write about the news item (4-level worksheet).
- Students share thoughts with partners.

INTRAPERSONAL

INTELLIGENCE

- Reflect on using the 4-level model.
- Share team insights about news items.
- Reflect on when the 4-level model would be helpful.

STAGE IV
TRANSFER

- Brainstorm a list of recent things that have happened to students.
- Introduce students to the 4-Level Reflection Model with a teacher example.
- Students turn to a neighbor and discuss an experience using the 4-level model.

AMPLIFY
STAGE II

The Model *Applied*

SkyLight Training and Publishing Inc.

How Am I Involved
and What Can I Do?

A CURRENT EVENTS LESSON WITH

Intrapersonal Intelligence

Lesson Procedures

☛ I like to call intrapersonal intelligence the introspective intelligence for it involves awareness about the self and feelings. Interpersonal intelligence looks outward and knows in and through relationships with others—it is the person-to-person way of knowing. Intrapersonal intelligence, on the other hand, looks inward and knows in and through investigating the self. As with interpersonal intelligence, intrapersonal intelligence needs all the other intelligences to express itself, and thus it is an integrator and synthesizer of the other ways of knowing.

INTRODUCTION

There is an ancient saying that goes, No man is an island entire in itself; every man is a piece of the continent, a part of the main. The truth of this is very evident in our world today—what happens in even one small corner of the world affects us all. In this current events lesson, students will be dialoguing with current events from around the world. The process of the lesson will lead them to various levels of self-discovery as they begin to see their connection to, and involvement in, these events. Inform students that they will be using their intrapersonal intelligence in the lesson and ask them to observe what this is like and what happens.

This lesson uses verbal/linguistic and interpersonal intelligences in addition to intrapersonal intelligence. Verbal/linguistic intelligence tools are employed when students read and discuss the news article. The interpersonal intelligence includes participating in cooperative groups and students listening to each other and effectively communicating their own feelings and points of view.

STAGE I

☛ Intrapersonal intelligence is awakened when we are in a situation that requires knowledge of the internal aspects of the self, such as our emotional state, thinking patterns, intuitions, creativity processes, and spiritual values or beliefs.

 **AWAKEN**

1. Tell the students to pretend they can travel twenty years into the future and ask, "What are you doing with your life?" Go around half of the class with each student answering the question.

These questions are designed to get students to look within themselves and begin to raise questions such as Who am I? and What am I about? In essence these questions help them reflect on a reflection about another reflection! When you see this happening and hear them reflecting deeply about their own lives, you know that intrapersonal intelligence has indeed been activated.

- Ask the class to reflect on what they heard. Prompt students to make up summary statements or observations about their answers to this question.

2. Now go around the other half of the class and ask, "What's the most important thing in your life right now ?"

3. Once again ask the class to reflect on what they heard. Prompt students to make up summary statements or observations about their answers to the question.

STAGE II

☛ Working with intrapersonal intelligence is especially difficult in our culture given our attitudes about introspection. On the one hand, we are often like a bunch of Mad Hatters rushing about because we are "late, late for a very important date." Our lives are so full of things that must be done, we often feel there is no time to stop and go inside ourselves. Thus we do not learn the specific skills of self-reflection and self-awareness. Furthermore, we carry with us a certain fear of what we might find if we look too deeply within. Some of this probably stems from popular images of the subconscious parts of our personality. These ideas about the subconscious have been fed by our impressions that Freudian analysis opens deep, dark closets full of terrible secrets and repressed problems from our childhood. We relate to the subconscious as something that is better left alone for it can open a Pandora's box!

In spite of all this bad press, researchers today are discovering that far from something to be feared, the inner worlds of the self are a vast storehouse of untapped potentials that are available to us if we learn the methods and techniques of accessing their riches. And the good news is the methods and techniques do exist and you do not have to be a spiritual guru or a neurological sophisticate to learn them!

 **AMPLIFY**

1. Tell the class that in this lesson they will have an opportunity to think about the daily news and how it affects their lives as well as how their lives affect the daily news.

2. Pass out two 4-Level Reflection Model worksheets to each student (see blackline, p. 164). Put the following questions from the model on the board or overhead and briefly explain the model to students:

   How am I involved? Where and how does the issue or concern touch my life? How does it make me feel? What are my thoughts and opinions about it?

   PMI (pluses, minuses, interesting; see glossary) What are the pluses of the issue (positive things about it)? What are its minuses (negative aspects)? What do I find interesting about the issue?

   My brainstorm of what could or should be done. If I was totally, completely, unconditionally in charge, what would I do? What do I think needs to happen in this situation? What action(s) should be taken?

   What I can do now? What steps could I take now (even if they seem very small and inconsequential) to bring about a resolution to this issue? (For example, I can recycle to do my small part to save the environment.)

   Explain that this model can help you think about an event on different levels.

3. Have each student write down three to five things they are struggling with in their life at the present moment. These items can be from school, family, church, friends, etc.

4. Explain that students will have a chance to talk about one of their issues with a partner using the 4-Level Reflection Model. Then, after they practice using the model, they will have an opportunity to apply it to current events in the world. Give them an example of an issue from your own life. (An example follows.)

SkyLight Training and Publishing Inc.

☞ When you, as the teacher, model how to do something for the students, try to simulate as close as possible the operation or exercise they will be performing later in the content part of the lesson. However, in the practice itself use familiar content so that students can give their attention to learning the skill you are teaching and not worry about getting some information they will need for a test later on.

EXAMPLE

Issue: Daughter's College Education

I. How Am I Involved?

- I want her to go to college.
- I think a year off between high school and college might be helpful to her.
- It is going to cost me a bundle.
- It makes me feel old. (It seems that just yesterday she was entering elementary school!)

II. PMI

Pluses (of college)

- Sets her up for a higher salary when she enters the workplace.
- It brings about a maturing and sense of responsibility for one's own life.
- Tight finances will force her to have a job to help pay.

Minuses (of college)

- She is not diligent with her high school studies and college is much more demanding.
- We have tight finances; therefore she may not be able to pick the school she wants most.
- Tight finances will force her to have a job to help pay.

Interesting

- If she took a year off between high school and college, she might be more ready for college.
- She is very interested in drama and other cultures.

III. What could or should be done?

- If I was in charge I'd put her in a school that uses cooperative learning extensively.
- I should be working more with her on her studies—helping her learn study methods for greater lesson success.

IV. What Now?

- We can start gathering information about different schools and costs.
- We can explore work-study programs which provide time in the real world.
- We can brainstorm job possibilities that utilize drama and multicultural interests.

☞ When the students are practicing using the 4-level reflection sheet with each other, it is important that you carefully monitor and observe their discussions to ensure that they are using the model and that they are staying on task. One way to do this is to have each person take notes as the other is speaking and then give those notes to his or her partner. This will also help students track and focus their reflections on the 4-level model.

☞ Working with a partner activates interpersonal intelligence skills. The sharing and discussion between them calls forth verbal/linguistic capacities.

5. Now have students turn to a partner and each take one of their issues through the 4-level reflection process. Be sure to instruct them to listen to each other and ask that they not make wisecracks while the other is speaking.

6. After both partners have had a chance to share their issue using the 4-level process, stop and briefly reflect with the whole class using questions such as the following:

- What was this like for you? What happened?
- What did you you notice about the different levels? How did they make you feel?
- What happened to your issue as you discussed it using these four levels?
- What questions do you have about using this model?

 **TEACH**

1. Tell students that they are now going to use the 4-level reflection process to have discussions with each other about the previous evening's news. Remind them that in thinking about and dialoguing with the news they can often gain a much deeper appreciation for what is going on in our world.

2. Now have students select a new partner, different from the person they talked with in the above practice conversation. Pass around a hat with news articles from the previous day's paper in it. Each pair is to select one news article from the hat.

3. Give the pairs an opportunity to read and understand the article together. When they have completed the reading, ask them to discuss it using questions such as the following:

- What are the main points of the article? Who is involved?
- What do we know about the background or history of this article?
- What are the main issues or points of view?
- How do I feel about this? What are my thoughts and opinions?

4. When the partners have had time to discuss the article with each other, instruct them to turn to their second 4-level reflection worksheet and to work individually, writing answers to the questions on the sheet. They must have something for each level of the reflection to succeed in this lesson, so watch carefully and give assistance to any students who seem to be having trouble.

5. When you notice that most students have completed the assignment, have them turn to their partner again and each share answers to the questions on the 4-level reflection worksheet. If time permits, have one pair join another pair and share their reflections on their article.

STAGE III

☞ Once students understand how to use the 4-Level Reflection Model, they can apply it to academic content.

This task again uses interpersonal intelligence skills to help students understand the item, necessary background information, its relevance and importance, and discuss initial feelings and thoughts about the item.

☞ In this time of sharing, students often learn a great deal from each other and about themselves. They begin to notice similarities and differences between themselves and their fellow students. They begin to develop a sense of security and/ or confidence about their own thoughts, opinions, and ideas. As they share, also encourage them to steal any good ideas or thoughts from each other and add these to their own reflections. This can help them understand that our so-called self-identity is really a combination of what goes on inside and what we experience in the outside world.

☞ It is important for them to write something for all four levels, even if they are not sure about what they are writing. Encourage them to trust their intuitions and record whatever pops into their head without evaluating it too much at this point. Some students may want to draw diagrams, pictures, or symbols to express their feelings. Others may want to write poetry or even turn their thoughts into a very short story. Anything they want to do is fine as long as they can demonstrate to you that they are in fact reflecting on all four levels of the model.

STAGE IV

☛ The goal of the transfer part of the lesson is to help students take what they have learned in the lesson and apply it in other areas of their schoolwork and in their everyday lives outside of school.

Two things take place in these reflections. They, first of all, discuss the pros and cons of the 4-level model and think about how to use it beyond this lesson and the classroom environment. This is an important transfer or bridging of the learning strategy. Second, they discuss insights and thoughts that the study of the news provoked. This dimension of reflection helps students learn to become thinkers rather than simply digesters of information.

TRANSFER

1. Reflect with the whole class on the use of the 4-level model to discuss the news. Ask questions like the following:

   - What did you find interesting about approaching the news in this way?

   - Which level was the easiest? hardest?

   - What do you like about this model? dislike?

2. Make a brainstorm list on the board or overhead of other times students think the 4-level process could be helpful to them.

3. Now have each pair share with the rest of the class an insight or thought they had about the news as they talked together about it in this manner.

SPIRAL ADAPTATIONS OF THE LESSON

Elementary School Level

1. Focus the lesson on learning to recognize pictures and names of key people in the news today and on being aware of how these people affect us.

2. Teach students to ask questions about what is happening in a story they already know, such as the "Three Little Pigs," "Goldilocks," etc. Have them make up questions they would ask the characters or a message they would give to the characters, if this were possible.

3. Show students pictures of key people in the news and tell a brief story about why they are in the news. Have students pretend they can ask the people questions or that they can give them a message—What would they say?

Middle School Level

1. Focus the lesson on listening to the evening news and understanding what is going on (including key people, places, and events).

2. Lead students to practice listening to a prerecorded curriculum event in the classroom from the previous day. Learn to recognize who was speaking, remember what they said, and recall what was going on in the classroom. Have students tell about how they feel and what they think about the tape.

3. Show students a video segment of the evening news from the night before. Recall people, places, and events with the class. Then have students write a letter to one of the people telling their feelings about what was reported on the news.

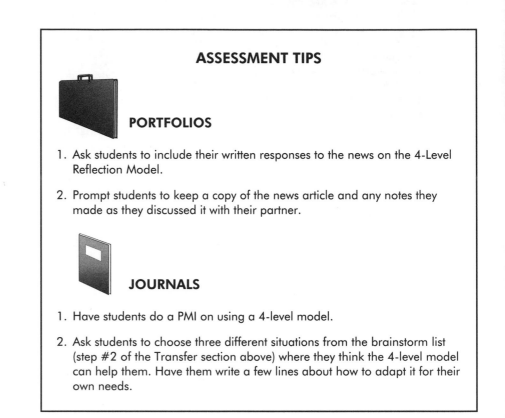

ASSESSMENT TIPS

PORTFOLIOS

1. Ask students to include their written responses to the news on the 4-Level Reflection Model.

2. Prompt students to keep a copy of the news article and any notes they made as they discussed it with their partner.

JOURNALS

1. Have students do a PMI on using a 4-level model.

2. Ask students to choose three different situations from the brainstorm list (step #2 of the Transfer section above) where they think the 4-level model can help them. Have them write a few lines about how to adapt it for their own needs.

Look to the Past . . .

Rethink a lesson you have completed recently. How would you restructure it to teach *for* and *with* intrapersonal intelligence?

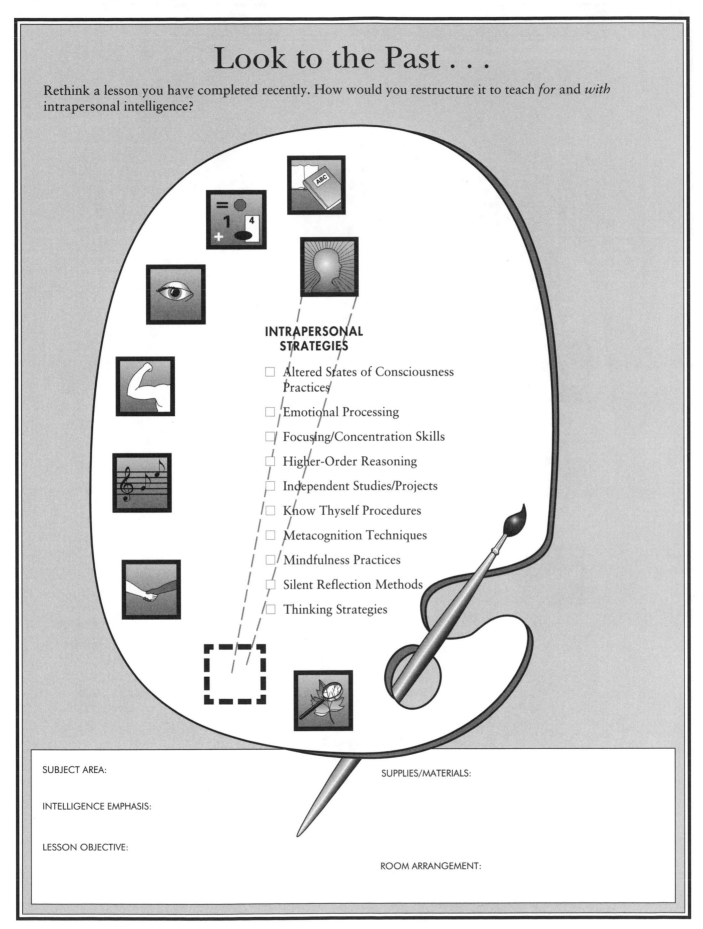

INTRAPERSONAL STRATEGIES

☐ Altered States of Consciousness Practices

☐ Emotional Processing

☐ Focusing/Concentration Skills

☐ Higher-Order Reasoning

☐ Independent Studies/Projects

☐ Know Thyself Procedures

☐ Metacognition Techniques

☐ Mindfulness Practices

☐ Silent Reflection Methods

☐ Thinking Strategies

SUBJECT AREA:

INTELLIGENCE EMPHASIS:

LESSON OBJECTIVE:

SUPPLIES/MATERIALS:

ROOM ARRANGEMENT:

Look to the Future . . .

Think about a lesson you have coming up in the near future. How would you structure it to teach *for* and *with* intrapersonal intelligence?

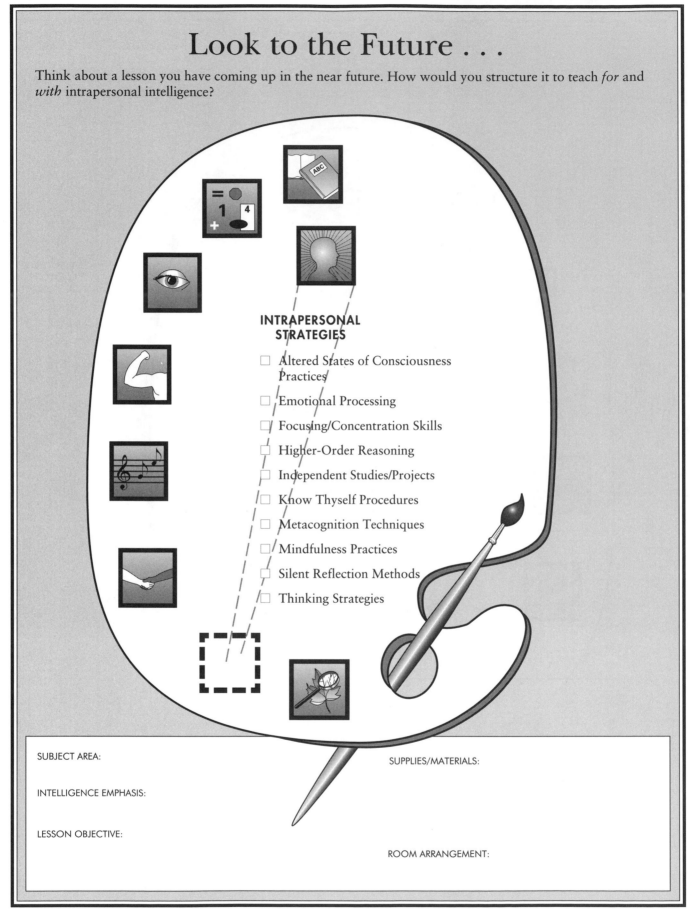

INTRAPERSONAL STRATEGIES

☐ Altered States of Consciousness Practices

☐ Emotional Processing

☐ Focusing/Concentration Skills

☐ Higher-Order Reasoning

☐ Independent Studies/Projects

☐ Know Thyself Procedures

☐ Metacognition Techniques

☐ Mindfulness Practices

☐ Silent Reflection Methods

☐ Thinking Strategies

SUBJECT AREA:

INTELLIGENCE EMPHASIS:

LESSON OBJECTIVE:

SUPPLIES/MATERIALS:

ROOM ARRANGEMENT:

Lesson Planning Ideas
Intrapersonal

HISTORY	MATHEMATICS	LANGUAGE ARTS	SCIENCE & HEALTH	GLOBAL STUDIES & GEOGRAPHY	FAMILY/CONSUMER SCIENCES, INDUSTRIAL TECHNOLOGY, & PE	FINE ARTS
Keep a journal about questions from your life that history might be able to answer	Track thinking patterns for different math problems	Write an autobiographical essay entitled My Life to Date	Design, implement, and evaluate a one-month Be Healthy project	Try awareness techniques* from other cultures	Discuss how different physical exercises make you feel	Draw yourself from different angles in a mirror
Do a PMI** analysis of famous historical decisions	Bridge math concepts beyond school using What? So What? Now What?**	Write an autobiographical essay entitled My Life in the Future	Conduct silent reflections on pictures of the solar system	List criteria of your ideal geography or climate and find it on a map	List how things learned in shop can help in your future life	Dance the different stages of your life's journey
Discuss this question: If I could be any historical figure who would I be and why?	Use guided imagery* to see complex story problems	Analyze literature for connections to our lives today	Write about If I could be any animal what would I be and why?	Discuss this question: How would I be different if I had grown up in another culture?	Write down and analyze conversations with your computer	Create a series of sculptures to express your moods
Write an essay on mistakes from the past that you will not repeat	Evaluate your strengths and weaknesses in understanding math	Write a new poem each day for a week answering the question Who am I?	Lead a series of I Become What I Behold* exercises	Learn focusing techniques* and see how each culture uses them	Watch yourself fix a meal and note everything that goes on	Imagine yourself as each character in a play
Imagine people from the past giving advice for living today	Watch mood changes as you do math problems and note causes	Imagine being a character in a story or play— What would you do?	Practice techniques for achieving deep relaxation* (e.g., breathing)	Keep a feelings diary as you read about current events	Imagine a skill and then try to do it exactly as you imagined	Carefully observe the effects of music on you

* See Glossary
** See Glossary and Appendix C

SkyLight Training and Publishing Inc.

TEACHING WITH
NATURALIST
INTELLIGENCE

THE EVOCATIVE POWER
OF NATURE FOR WRITING

A Language Arts Lesson:
Secondary School Level

Lesson Palette: *Naturalist* Emphasis

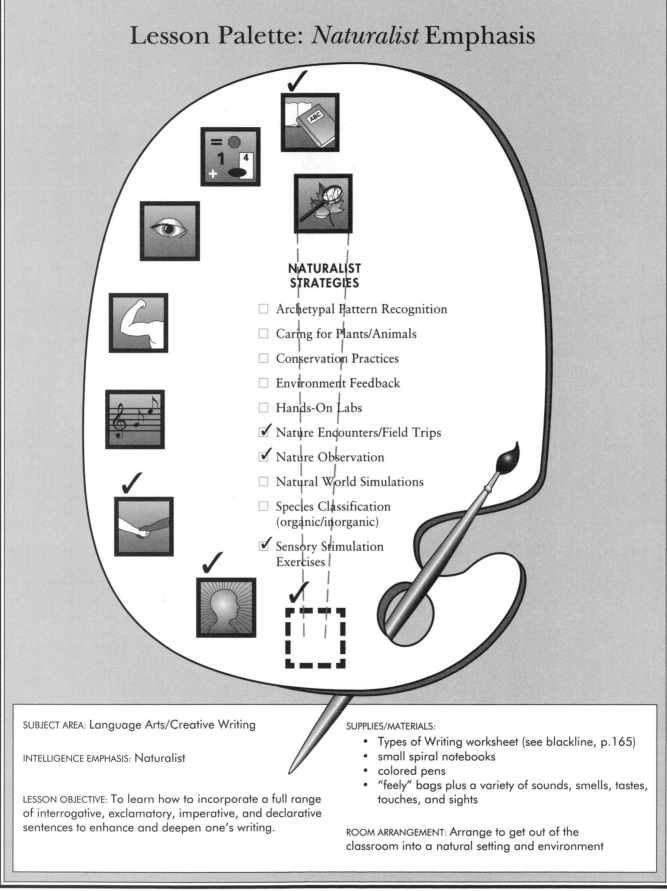

NATURALIST STRATEGIES

- ☐ Archetypal Pattern Recognition
- ☐ Caring for Plants/Animals
- ☐ Conservation Practices
- ☐ Environment Feedback
- ☐ Hands-On Labs
- ☑ Nature Encounters/Field Trips
- ☑ Nature Observation
- ☐ Natural World Simulations
- ☐ Species Classification (organic/inorganic)
- ☑ Sensory Stimulation Exercises

SUBJECT AREA: Language Arts/Creative Writing

INTELLIGENCE EMPHASIS: Naturalist

LESSON OBJECTIVE: To learn how to incorporate a full range of interrogative, exclamatory, imperative, and declarative sentences to enhance and deepen one's writing.

SUPPLIES/MATERIALS:
- Types of Writing worksheet (see blackline, p.165)
- small spiral notebooks
- colored pens
- "feely" bags plus a variety of sounds, smells, tastes, touches, and sights

ROOM ARRANGEMENT: Arrange to get out of the classroom into a natural setting and environment

THE LESSON . . .

STAGE I
AWAKEN

Awaken naturalist intelligence by immersing
the self in the full sensory experience of the
natural world including plants, animals,
weather conditions, water, forests, inorganic
matter, etc., from the microscopic world to
what can be perceived with the naked eye,
the sense of taste, touch, smell, sound, and
the inner senses of the human spirit (e.g.,
being moved and touched by nature).

NATURALIST

INTELLIGENCE

STAGE III
TEACH

Teach for and with
naturalist intelligence by
using the specific tools of
this intelligence and
applying them to help
learn the content, acquire
specific knowledge, and
achieve the lesson's goals
and/or objectives.

STAGE IV
TRANSFER

Transfer naturalist
intelligence to life by
discussing the intelligence
tools employed, finding
applications for the
intelligence and the content
beyond the lesson or unit
to other curricular areas,
and finally integrating it
into the task of living in
the world outside of the
classroom.

Amplify naturalist intelligence through
practice recognizing members of a species
(organic and inorganic), learning to distin-
guish differences among members of the
same species, and understanding other
neighboring species (who are similar but
different). The naturalist intelligence is also
enhanced in and through regular interactions with nature such as caring for or
taming animals or growing and nurturing
plants.

AMPLIFY
STAGE II

The Model

SkyLight Training and Publishing Inc.

...AT A GLANCE

STAGE I
AWAKEN

- Lesson Introduction: Creative writing through encounters with nature
- The teacher passes around several "feely" bags containing objects from nature:

  The students cannot look in the bags— only touch what is in them.

  The students guess what the object is.

NATURALIST

INTELLIGENCE

STAGE III
TEACH

- The teacher introduces the four basic types of writing worksheet to the students.
- Students go outside to a natural setting and fully experience all that it has to offer using the five senses.
- Students write about their experience using the basic types of writing.

TRANSFER
STAGE IV

- Reflect on the experience and process of being evoked by nature and trying to write about the experience
- Reflect on the four types of writing
- Reflect on where else the four types of sentences can be (and *are*) used beyond school

- Teacher exposes students (who have their eyes closed) to a variety of sounds, smells, tastes, touches, and sights.
- Students talk with partners about what was evoked by the experience (e.g. thoughts, associations, images, colors, other people, etc.).
- As one partner speaks, the other records what he or she is saying.

AMPLIFY
STAGE II

The Model *Applied*

The Evocative Power
of Nature for Writing

A LANGUAGE ARTS LESSON WITH

Naturalist Intelligence

Lesson Procedures

INTRODUCTION

The natural world is full of innumerable things that can evoke the full range of our five senses as well as inner feelings, intuitions, memories, spiritual insight, and a profound sense of connectedness and unity. In this lesson students spend time in nature, allowing these things to be evoked within themselves. They then use this experience as a springboard to creative writing. The lesson focuses on incorporating the five foundational kinds of writing (descriptive, interrogative, declarative, exclamatory, and imperative) into students' creative writing. They will focus on using their naturalist intelligence to help them deepen and enrich their writing.

In addition to the naturalist intelligence, verbal/linguistic intelligence shares a secondary focus in this lesson—students will actually be writing about their experiences in nature. Throughout the lesson they will also work with a partner, so interpersonal intelligence is involved as well. Intrapersonal intelligence gets into the act, as students are asked to become introspective and be aware of nature's impact on them via the traditional five senses, but also how nature affects the inner world of the self.

☞ The realm of the naturalist intelligence is the realm of understanding, appreciating, and enjoying the natural world. Persons who exhibit strength in the naturalist intelligence are very much at home in nature. They demonstrate expertise in recognizing and classifying the many different species (both organic and inorganic). Famous people who exemplify the naturalist intelligence include Charles Darwin, Meriwether Lewis and William Clark, James Audubon, and Carolus Linnaeus.

AWAKEN

STAGE I

☞ The naturalist intelligence is awakened in and through various sensory encounters with the natural world including plants, animals, weather conditions, water,

1. Tell students that since they will be using their naturalist intelligence in the lesson, you are going to spend a view minutes trying to stimulate or trigger the centers in the brain that are involved in

forests, inorganic matter, etc., from the microscopic world to what can be perceived with the naked eye, the sense of taste, touch, smell, sound, and the inner senses of the human spirit (e.g., being moved and touched by nature).

The direct experience of nature tends to catalyze certain neural centers and networks within the human brain. Some researchers believe that certain clusters of cells within our brains are devoted *exclusively* to the recognition, appreciation, and understanding of the natural world as opposed to the world of human creation!

working with this intelligence. Tell students that you have put together several nature "feely" bags that you're going to pass around the room. (Note: Items in the bags could include a rabbit's foot, tree bark, a lump of dirt, a feather, various parts of different kinds of plants, different kinds of rocks, fur, and so on. If you have the time you could also have some "smelly" bags in which you have placed natural objects that have a distinct odor and have student encounter nature via their olfactory senses.)

2. Start passing the bags around the room. Tell students not to look into the bags. Students are to experience what is in the different bags, seeing if they can recognize them; however they are not to speak this out loud. They are simply to know for themselves.

3. After the bags have been around the whole class, empty the bags so students can see the objects. Have students share with their neighbors what happened to them as they encountered the different objects in the bags: What got awakened or stimulated as a result of this exercise?

4. Ask several groups to share some of their observations and experiences with the whole class.

STAGE II

☞ Although I mentioned some so-called famous naturalists in my earlier comments, some less famous examples would include almost any preschooler or kindergartner and their fascination with, desire to explore, and compulsion to get dirty *in* and *with* the natural world! As we get older we tend to get further and further away from the firsthand experience with and exploration of the natural world. As we move into adulthood, we frequently spend twenty-four hours a day living and moving and having our being in the proverbial, humanly-created concrete jungle.

Nevertheless, the restimulation and possible recovery of the childhood wonder with nature (and the potential restimulation of our naturalist intelligence) is as close as the nearest natural setting, be it a national or local park, an arboretum, a botanical garden, or even a neighborhood nursery or gardening center.

☞ The purpose of this five senses exercise is to give students a chance to practice a process for activating the senses—the very

 **AMPLIFY**

1. Have each student find a partner that they will work with during the lesson. Remind them that the goal of the lesson is to enhance, expand, and deepen their creative writing by getting in touch with the sensory world. But first let them practice the basic process they will use in the lesson.

2. Have students arrange their chairs so they face in opposite directions but they are seated side-by-side, so that they have easy access to each other's ears for quiet conversation. Each student is to have paper and pencil.

3. Have students decide that one of them is person A and other is person B. Instruct them to close their eyes (no peeking!). Tell them they are now going to be exposed to a variety of sounds, smells, tastes, touches, and sights.

Partner A will record what was evoked (e.g., thoughts, associations, images, colors, other people, memories, etc.) in partner B through the sounds, smells, tastes, touches, and sights. Partner B will do the same for partner A. They will bounce back and forth between A and B with one person speaking, sharing what was evoked and the other person recording what their partner is saying. (Note: The focus is *not* to guess what the sound, smell, etc. is but rather to be aware of the feelings, associations, images, etc. that are evoked.)

process they will use later in the lesson to enhance their creative writing.

4. Proceed quickly through each of the five senses providing an experience first for person A then for person B. Some examples follow:

Sense	Person A	Person B
Sound	xylophone	tapping fingers
Touch	velvet	sandpaper
Smell	sage	perfume
Taste	chocolate	salted nut
Sight	weird object	mirror

After each experience, one partner speaks about his or her associations, feelings, images, memories, colors, etc. that were evoked by the experience. *Without making any comments,* the other partner is simply to record what his or her partner has said.

5. Ask several partners to share with the whole class what happened as they worked with each other: What did you discover about your five senses?

 **TEACH**

1. Pass out the Types of Writing Worksheet (see blackline, p. 165). Explain the different types to students and give some examples of the importance of each. Or have them come up with examples of when they use each type in communication with others.

- Declarative writing is a simple statement of fact. (For example, I'll meet you at the corner cafe.)

- Interrogative writing is a statement of a question. (For example, Should we meet at the cafe or elsewhere?)

- Imperative writing is a statement of a command to someone else. (For example, Be at the cafe no later than 11:00 a.m.)

- Exclamatory writing is an emphatic statement or one of exclamation. (For example, We had a fabulous time when we met at the cafe!)

2. Now tell the class they are going to have a chance to work with and incorporate these different types of sentences through an experience with the natural world. Give the class the following directions:

a. Go outside with your partner to a *natural* spot on which you

STAGE II

☞ This traditional academic content part of the lesson could either be a review of previously studied information or a lesson to introduce the sentence types as new information. Feel free to utilize textbook information describing the basic sentence types (be they four or forty!).

☞ The whole purpose of taking students outside is to expose them to nature as an evocateur of their creative writing capacities. Within our natural world are vast resources that can touch us deeply and in so doing help us enhance, deepen, and amplify our writing.

☞ If it is impossible to take students outside into nature (which is best to fully activate the naturalist intelligence from a neurological standpoint), you must find some way to bring nature in—whether it be in a video or having actual representations of the natural world present in the classroom (e.g., you may have various nature stations which students visit during the process of the lesson).

both agree. (The key is to be in a *natural* setting *not* something made by humans!)

b. As in the practice session earlier, have one partner speak while the other records and then switch roles.

c. Once you are settled, spend a few minutes in silence just being in this place. Ask yourselves: What am I hearing? What am I smelling? What catches my eyes? What textures do I see or feel?

☛ Do not let students get too hung up on having a response in every box of the worksheet; however, make sure you encourage them to fill in as many as possible so they will have more to draw on when they get into the creative writing. In their conversations with each other, encourage the partners to stay at the feeling level as it relates to the five senses.

d. After spending several minutes of just being there, the recorder should ask his or her partner to talk out loud about what he or she is experiencing with the five senses. Record his or her sensory experience in the appropriate place on the worksheet chart and under the appropriate type of sentence. As necessary, use the questions on the worksheet to get your partner to express his or her experience of each sense in the four ways.

(Note: Students may want to focus on one sense at a time with each person speaking in the four ways back and forth and then move on to another. It is not necessary that every single box on the chart be filled. They should just do as many as possible in the given time.)

e. After each partner has completed responding to as many of the questions for the different types of sentences as possible, stop and give the Types of Writing Worksheet to your partner. Read it over, asking the partner for clarification of anything that is not clear.

☛ When they are doing their writing remind them to use the information their partner recorded on the worksheet to help them create a juicy piece!

f. Now take individual time to write about your experience in nature. Use the worksheet as a guide. The goal of the writing is to include sentences which express experiences from the perspective of each of the senses as well as each of the sentence type columns. Use the sensory experience and the sentence type to create an interesting and compelling piece—something that someone else will really want to read!

g. When you have completed your writing, exchange your piece with your partner. Read what your partner has written and, in turn, give feedback using the following starter phrases:

What really grabs my attention in your writing is . . .

As I read your piece I was surprised by . . .

One thing I think you could do to make this a stronger piece is . . .

If you had to give your piece to someone else to read, to whom would you give it and why?

What title would you give your piece?

TRANSFER

☞ The goal of the transfer part of the lesson is to help students find the relevance of the lesson for their own lives. Here we are concerned with helping them go beyond the lesson itself, into other curricular areas, and finally into their lives beyond the classroom.

☞ The reflection on the process of being evoked by nature will help students get a better understanding of one aspect of the naturalist intelligence.

☞ The reflection on the writing process is intended to help students see direct connections between this lesson and the use of these four sentence types to enrich their communication (both written and spoken) in all aspects of their lives.

1. Reflect with the students on the experience and process of being evoked by nature and writing about the experience using the following questions:

   • What happened to you as you allowed yourself to be impacted and evoked by nature? What was most interesting about this experience for you?

   • What surprised you? What was exciting?

   • How did this experience help you with your writing? What was most difficult?

   • What did you learn in this process that will help you in the future when you are involved in creative writing?

2. Reflect on the four type of sentences:

   • Which of the four types of sentences do you like the most? Why? Which do you dislike? Why?

   • Where (beyond school) are you aware of these kinds of sentences being used?

   • Where in your life do think the conscious use of these sentences can help you enhance and deepen your verbal and written communication?

SPIRAL ADAPTATIONS OF THE LESSON

Elementary School Level

1. Create a page of faces which show a whole range of possible feelings, such as sad, confused, angry, etc. When you are doing the amplifying stage, the partner circles the appropriate face for his or her partner as the partner reacts to the five senses experiences.

2. Keep the lesson on the speaking level rather than writing. Tell the children that when we are talking to each other, there are at least four different ways we talk: we ask questions (interrogative), we tell people what we want them to do (imperative), we explain things (declarative), we tell about our strong feelings (exclamatory). Show a picture to go with each type.

3. Demonstrate the four ways of speaking and ask the children to point to the appropriate picture. Take the children outside and give them several nature-based scenarios to role play. Have them practice speaking in the four ways as if they were objects in

nature (e.g., speak as the plant that wants some water or as the squirrel that is wondering about how to jump from one tree to the next.).

Middle School Level

1. The awakening and amplifying levels can be used as they are presented in the lesson procedures above.

2. In the teaching part of the lesson, focus the lesson on human relations and human relating. Talk about four things we can do to improve our relating with our friends, parents, and teachers:

   - We can ask questions to make sure we understand.

   - We can tell others what we want them to do.

   - We can carefully explain and describe our own thoughts and feelings.

   - We can express our strong feelings in ways that make others take notice.

3. Take the students outside into a natural environment and present them with a potential environmental problem about the space you have chosen. Have students, in groups of three or four, prepare statements from the four ways of relating that could make a difference and resolve the problem (e.g., What are the key questions that should be asked? What are the things people should do to resolve this problem?, etc.).

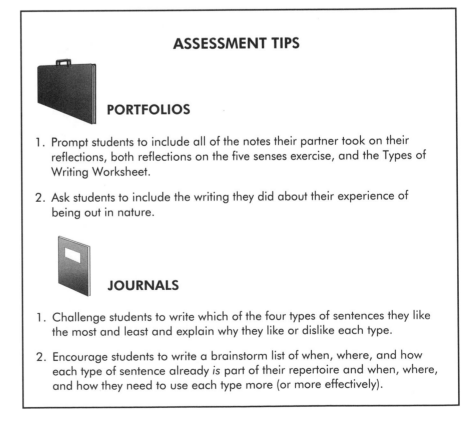

ASSESSMENT TIPS

PORTFOLIOS

1. Prompt students to include all of the notes their partner took on their reflections, both reflections on the five senses exercise, and the Types of Writing Worksheet.

2. Ask students to include the writing they did about their experience of being out in nature.

JOURNALS

1. Challenge students to write which of the four types of sentences they like the most and least and explain why they like or dislike each type.

2. Encourage students to write a brainstorm list of when, where, and how each type of sentence already *is* part of their repertoire and when, where, and how they need to use each type more (or more effectively).

Look to the Past . . .

Rethink a lesson you have completed recently. How would you restructure it to teach *for* and *with* naturalist intelligence?

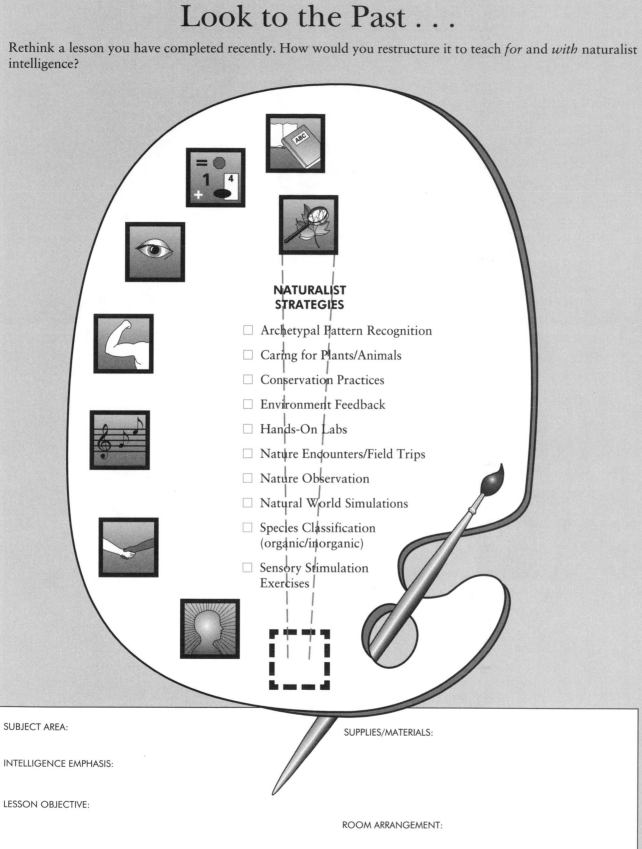

NATURALIST STRATEGIES

☐ Archetypal Pattern Recognition

☐ Caring for Plants/Animals

☐ Conservation Practices

☐ Environment Feedback

☐ Hands-On Labs

☐ Nature Encounters/Field Trips

☐ Nature Observation

☐ Natural World Simulations

☐ Species Classification (organic/inorganic)

☐ Sensory Stimulation Exercises

SUBJECT AREA:

INTELLIGENCE EMPHASIS:

LESSON OBJECTIVE:

SUPPLIES/MATERIALS:

ROOM ARRANGEMENT:

Look to the Future . . .

Think about a lesson you have coming up in the near future. How would you structure it to teach *for* and *with* naturalist intelligence?

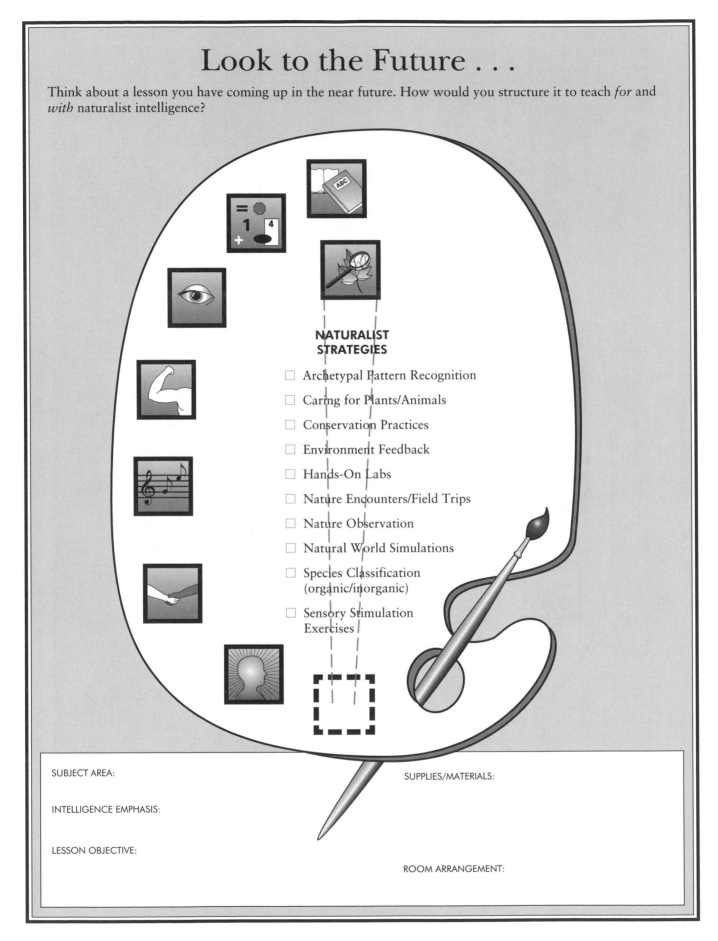

NATURALIST STRATEGIES

☐ Archetypal Pattern Recognition

☐ Caring for Plants/Animals

☐ Conservation Practices

☐ Environment Feedback

☐ Hands-On Labs

☐ Nature Encounters/Field Trips

☐ Nature Observation

☐ Natural World Simulations

☐ Species Classification (organic/inorganic)

☐ Sensory Stimulation Exercises

SUBJECT AREA:

INTELLIGENCE EMPHASIS:

LESSON OBJECTIVE:

SUPPLIES/MATERIALS:

ROOM ARRANGEMENT:

LESSON PLANNING IDEAS
Naturalist

HISTORY	MATHEMATICS	LANGUAGE ARTS	SCIENCE & HEALTH	GLOBAL STUDIES & GEOGRAPHY	FAMILY/CONSUMER SCIENCES, INDUSTRIAL TECHNOLOGY, & PE	FINE ARTS
Recognize and interpret historical trends (à la Toynbee)	Work story problems based on or dealing with patterns in nature	Nature scene re-creations or simulations for literature and poetry	Classify different foods for healthy diet planning	Environmental representations for different cultures	Grow fruits, vegetables, and herbs and use them in preparing a meal	Compose using sounds from nature and the environment
Understand how natural events have influenced history	Use nature manipulatives in math problem solving	Poetic or descriptive essay writing based on nature experiences	Experience past scientific experiments firsthand (Do them!)	Grow and/or taste foods from various cultures	Experience (via field trips) the process of making cloth from natural materials	Recognize and re-create visual images of natural patterns
Create analogies between historical and natural events	Graph positive and negative influences on the environment	Learn and practice using the vocabulary of nature and the naturalist	Keep a diary of the natural processes of your own body	Study the influence of climate and/or geography on cultural development	Create useful objects for the home, classroom, or office using *only* natural products	Create dances which "embody" or demonstrate patterns in nature
Study how animals have affected history and historical trends	Understand the mathematical patterns of nature	Understand influences of climate and/or environment on authors	Use of various naturalist taxonomies on nature field trips	Re-create multimedia experiences of the natural environments of different cultures	Play outdoor games that use natural objects and that are based on natural patterns	Design full-blown dramatic enactments of natural processes
Study the lives of famous naturalists and their impact on history	Calculation problems based on nature and natural processes	Creative story-writing using animal characters and their characteristics	Use cognitive organizers to explore and understand scientific processes	Study animals, insects, etc. from different parts of the world	Create virtual reality encounters with natural phenomena on a computer	Make montages or collages incorporating natural products

EPILOGUE

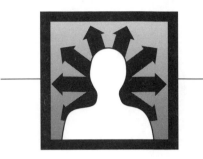

Epilogue

The old Chinese proverb that questions whether it is better to give a man a fish for today or teach him the art of fishing to prepare him for a lifetime applies quite well to the contemporary task of education, and especially at the point of teaching *for, with,* and *about* multiple intelligences. One of the major purposes of school should be to develop as full a range of intellectual capacities in students as possible. The good news about teaching *with* multiple intelligences is that it is not an add-on to already overfilled curricula. Teaching *with* multiple intelligences can and should be happening every day in and through whatever curricula we are teaching. However, we must keep our attention in the right place; namely, on the development of students' fullest potential as human beings. This includes their ability to perform on various standardized tests which our culture deems an important part of education. However, I believe we can have our cake and eat it too, so to speak. Students will more thoroughly learn the things we are trying to teach if we provide them the opportunity to develop the full range of their intellectual capacities and to use their multiple ways of knowing in the learning task, rather than if we only permit them to learn in the more traditional verbal/linguistic and logical/mathematical ways.

In order to be successful in this endeavor, our teaching *for, with,* and *about* the intelligences needs to match the pattern of the natural development and growth of the intelligences. Each intelligence begins with what Howard Gardner calls *raw patterning ability*. This stage involves the ability to perform certain simple tasks that are foundational to the operation of a given intelligence—learning certain motor skills such as walking, running, and jumping for bodily/kinesthetic intelligence or learning the alphabet and how to speak for verbal/linguistic intelligence. As the child develops, the raw patterning of an intelligence moves to a greater level of complexity in what Gardner calls a *symbol system.* Here the basic skills of an intelligence are combined in more complex patterns in order to give expressions of meaning. For example, the ability to make different tones expresses itself as a melody in musical/rhythmic intelligence or the ability to draw different shapes expresses itself in a picture with color and perspective in visual/spatial intelligence. The next stage of development builds on this symbol system stage and represents itself in what Gardner calls a *notational system.* Each of the intelligences has its own language—a language that can be taught, learned, and transmitted to others. These are things that can be recorded in some form for posterity, such as musical composition and performance (musical/rhythmic intelligence); consensus building and an understanding of group process (interpersonal intelligence); or the conscious use of inductive and deductive thought processes (logical/mathematical intelligence). The final stage of the development of an intelligence is the *vocational or avocational pursuit stage.* The mature expression of intellectual development involves its embodiment in particular career paths of societal service roles such as those mentioned in the introductory chapter to this book.

In terms of the developmental journey of the human being, the raw patterning stage is generally the earliest part of one's childhood (infancy and before school). The symbol system stage is represented by the early years of schooling (preschool, kindergarten, and the first years of elementary school). The notational system stage generally occurs in the late elementary school years and in the middle school or junior high years, and early secondary schooling. The vocational or avocational pursuit stage of development can generally be associated with the late secondary and college years, as well as adulthood.

In addition to these developmental considerations, all students possess all of the intelligences at each stage of their development, although not all of them are developed to the same degree at a given time. Therefore, certain kinds of assessment activities are needed to help us paint a profile of a given student's intelligence strengths and weaknesses so that we can help them design strategies for strengthening their weaker intelligences and learn how to use their stronger intelligences to enhance and deepen their learning.

In *Eight Ways of Knowing* I proposed five experimental approaches for assessing a student's intellectual profile. Each of these suggests that the task of assessing an intelligence profile is primarily a matter of acute observation of students involved in various kinds of activities and/or learning tasks. A summary of these follows:

1. **Student Intelligence Watch.** This is a checklist of various behaviors that often manifest themselves in the classroom and may (especially if you observe them as a regular part of a student's life) indicate certain ways a student is trying to enhance his or her

learning. These include such things as the student who is always getting up out of his or her seat, the doodler, the hummer, the perpetual questioner, the silent one, etc.

2. **Intelligence Skill Games.** These provide students with a choice of games to play. These could include such intelligence-specific things as Pictionary, charades, crossword puzzles, tune or music recognition, etc. It is important to observe not only which game(s) they choose, but *what they do* as they are playing.

3. **Intelligence Foci Watching.** This involves showing students a complex movie or a play in which multiple intelligence capacities are clearly portrayed and/or utilized, such as any of the *Star Wars* series, Disney cartoons like *Bambi*, or *The Miracle Worker*. After the film or play, lead them in a discussion on what struck them. Notice the points—the action scenes, the musical sound track, colors, symbols, emotions—that captured their attention.

4. **Complex Problem Solving.** Watch *what* students do when given a problem to solve—one that they really care about solving. You can tell a great deal about their intelligence patterns as you catch them in the act of problem solving. Remember, the answer itself is not as important as *how* they approach it!

5. **Inventing.** Give students inventing, designing, or creating tasks to perform, making sure that the full spectrum of intelligence tools is available for them to use. Then, again, notice to which kinds of tools they are drawn to, and again, *what* they do with the tools once they have them.

Howard Gardner believes that it takes about ten hours of careful observation of students involved in activities such as these to begin sensing a profile of their intelligence strengths and weaknesses. I believe that it is also crucial to mention that this profile will change as students learn about their multiple intelligences and how to use them in daily lessons and in their lives beyond school. The observation must be ongoing. The promise, of course, is that we as teachers can find strategies for coaxing students to step beyond their limits and become all that they can be!

I wish you an exciting and wonder-filled adventure as you journey into these realms of amplified ways of knowing and being!

LESSON PROCESSING BLACKLINES

APPENDIX

A

Multiple Intelligences
Toolbox Descriptions

Verbal/Linguistic Intelligence

Creative Writing—writing original pieces without boundaries

Formal Speaking—making verbal presentations to others

Humor/Jokes—creating puns, limericks, and jokes on academic topics

Impromptu Speaking—instantly speaking on a randomly drawn topic

Journal/Diary Keeping—tracing and keeping track of one's own thoughts and ideas

Poetry—creating one's own poetry and reading and appreciating others' poetry

Reading—studying written materials on a concept, idea, or process

Storytelling/Story Creation—making up and telling stories about any topic one is studying

Verbal Debate—presenting both sides of an issue in a convincing manner

Vocabulary—learning new words and practicing using them accurately in regular communication

Logical/Mathematical Intelligence

Abstract Symbols/Formulas—designing meaningful summary notation systems for different processes or knowledge content

Calculation—using specified steps, operations, processes, formulas, and equations to solve a problem

Deciphering Codes—understanding and communicating with symbolic language

Forcing Relationships—creating meaningful connections between noncongruent ideas

Graphic/Cognitive Organizers—working with logical thought maps such as webs, Venn diagrams, classification matrices, ranking ladders, etc.

Logic/Pattern Games—creating puzzles that challenge others to find a hidden rationale or pattern

Number Sequences/Patterns—investigating numerical facts or gathering and analyzing statistics on a topic

Outlining—inventing point-by-point logical explanations for items

Problem Solving—listing appropriate procedures for problem-solving situations

Syllogisms—making *if . . . , then . . .* logical deductions about a topic

Visual/Spatial Intelligence

Active Imagination—finding connections between visual designs (or patterns) and prior experiences (or knowledge)

Color/Texture Schemes—associating colors and textures with various concepts, ideas, or processes

Drawing—creating graphic representations of concepts, ideas, or processes being studied (e.g., diagrams, illustrations, flowcharts, etc.)

Guided Imagery/Visualizing—creating mental pictures or images of a concept, idea, or process (e.g., characters in a story, a period of history, a scientific process)

Mind Mapping—creating visual webs of written information

Montage/Collage—designing a collection of pictures to show various aspects or dimensions of a concept, idea, or process

Painting—using paints or colored markers to express understanding of concepts, ideas, or processes (e.g., mural creation)

Patterns/Designs—creating abstract patterns and designs to represent the relationships between different concepts, ideas, or processes

Pretending/Fantasy—creating fun, new scenarios in the mind based on factual information

Sculpting—creating clay models to demonstrate understanding of concepts, ideas, or processes

Bodily/Kinesthetic Intelligence

Body Language/Physical Gestures—"embodying" meaning, interpretation, or understanding of an idea in physical movement

Body Sculpture/Tableaus—arranging (sculpting) a group of people to express an idea, concept, or process

Dramatic Enactment—creating a mini-drama that shows the dynamic interplay of various concepts, ideas, or processes

Folk/Creative Dance—choreographing a dance that demonstrates a concept, idea, or process

Gymnastic Routines—designing an orchestrated flow of physical movement which embodies relationships and connections with a topic

Human Graph—standing along a continuum to express agreement or understanding of a concept, idea, or process

Inventing—making or building something that demonstrates a concept, idea, or process (e.g., a model to show how something works)

Physical Exercise/Martial Arts—creating physical routines that others perform so that they may learn concepts, ideas, or processes

Role Playing/Mime—performing skits or charades to show understanding of concepts, ideas, or processes

Sports Games—creating a contest or game based on specific knowledge about a concept, idea, or process

Musical/Rhythmic Intelligence

Environmental Sounds—using the natural sounds that are related to the object, concept, or process being studied (e.g., weather conditions, geographical locations, animals)

Instrumental Sounds—employing musical instruments to produce sounds for a lesson (e.g., background accompaniment, enhancements for the teaching)

Music Composition/Creation—composing and creating music to communicate understanding of a concept, idea, or process (e.g., the stages of a cell dividing)

Music Performance—creating presentations or reports in which music and rhythm play a central role

Percussion Vibrations—using vibrations or beats to communicate a concept, idea, or process to others and the self

Rapping—using raps to help communicate or to remember certain concepts, ideas, or processes

Rhythmic Patterns—producing rhythms and beats to show the various aspects of a concept, idea, or process

Singing/Humming—creating songs about an academic topic or finding existing songs that complement a topic

Tonal Patterns—recognizing the tone dimension(s) of a topic (e.g., sounds a computer makes)

Vocal Sounds/Tones—producing sounds with one's vocal cords to illustrate a concept, idea, or process

Interpersonal Intelligence

Collaborative Skills Teaching—recognizing and learning the social skills needed for effective person-to-person relating

Cooperative Learning Strategies—using structured teamwork for academic learning

Empathy Practices—expressing understanding from someone else's standpoint or life experience

Giving Feedback—offering honest, sensitive input on one's performance or about one's opinion(s)

Group Projects—investigating a topic with others in teams

Intuiting Others' Feelings—second-guessing what someone else is feeling or experiencing in a given situation

Jigsaw—dividing the learning and teaching of a topic into distinct segments so that students can learn from and teach each other

Person-to-Person Communication—focusing on how people relate and how to improve their relating

Receiving Feedback—accepting another's input or reaction to one's performance or opinions

Sensing Others' Motives—exploring a topic by discovering why others acted in a certain way or made certain decisions

Intrapersonal Intelligence

Altered States of Consciousness Practices—learning to shift one's mood or awareness into an optimal state

Emotional Processing—becoming aware of the affective dimensions (i.e., How does it make me feel?) of something one is studying

Focusing/Concentration Skills—learning the ability to focus one's mind on a single idea or task

Higher-Order Reasoning—moving from memorizing facts to synthesizing, integrating, and applying

Independent Studies/Projects—working alone to expresses feelings and thoughts on a topic

Know Thyself Procedures—finding personal implications or applications of classroom learning for one's personal life

Metacognition Techniques—thinking about one's thinking (i.e., tracing the various processes and steps used)

Mindfulness Practices—paying conscious attention to one's life experience (the opposite of mindlessness or "living on automatic pilot")

Silent Reflection Methods—working with reflection tools such as reflective journals, thinking logs, learning diaries, etc.

Thinking Strategies—learning what thinking patterns to use for what task

Naturalist Intelligence

Archetypal Pattern Recognition—discovering the repeating, standard patterns and designs of nature that manifest themselves throughout the universe

Caring for Plants/Animals—completing projects that involve caring for and/or training animals, insects, other organisms, and/or growing natural things

Conservation Practices—participating in projects that care for and preserve the natural environment (including its animals)

Environment Feedback—understanding and appreciating the environment and tuning in to the natural feedback coming from the environment

Hands-On Labs—performing experiments or activities that use objects from the natural world

Nature Encounters/Field Trips—going outside for firsthand experiences in nature and/or bringing nature in via videos, objects, animals, plants, etc.

Nature Observation—participating in observation activities such as bird-watching, geological exploration, keeping nature journals

Nature World Simulations—re-creating or representing nature in some form (e.g., dioramas, montages, photographs, drawings, nature rubbings, etc.)

Species Classification (organic/inorganic)—working with classification matrices to understand characteristics of natural objects

Sensory Stimulation Exercises—exposing the senses to nature's sounds, smells, tastes, touches, and sights

Lesson Design Palette

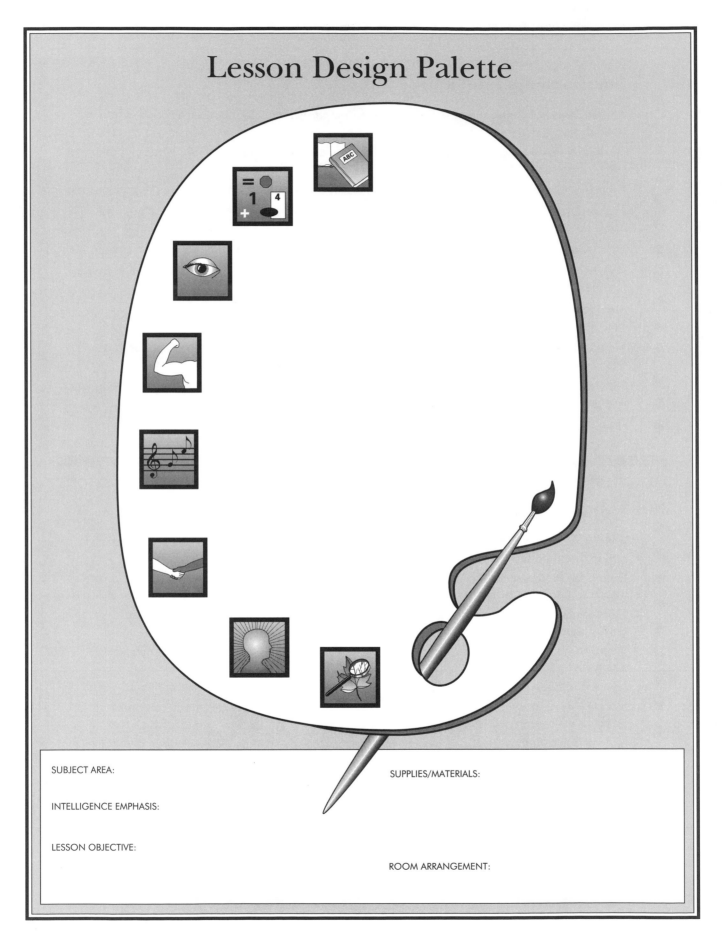

SUBJECT AREA:

SUPPLIES/MATERIALS:

INTELLIGENCE EMPHASIS:

LESSON OBJECTIVE:

ROOM ARRANGEMENT:

Lesson Plan Staging Model

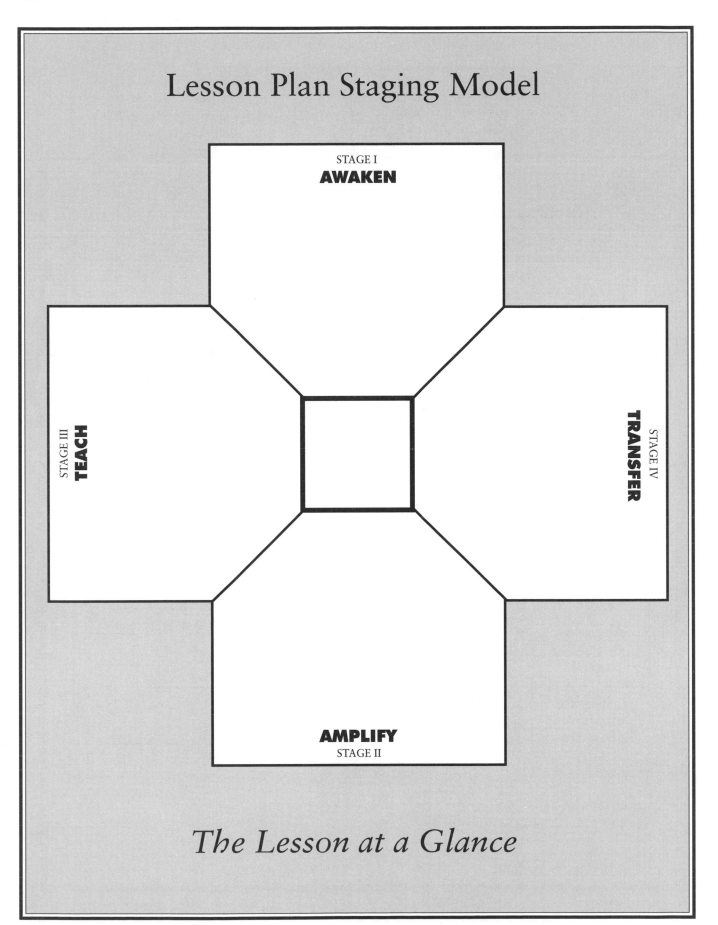

The Lesson at a Glance

Models for Student Journals

Note: Journals can involve different modes of reflecting including writing, drawing, painting, sculpting, role playing, dancing, etc.

THINKING LOGS (to process lesson content)

The main thing I'll remember is . . .
A new insight or discovery is . . .
I really understood . . .; I'm really confused about . . .
A learning I can use beyond school is . . .
Connections I'm making with other things I know are . . .

BEFORE AND AFTER SCENARIOS (to process impact of a lesson)

Analyze the impact of a unit or lesson on you using this chart.

	BEFORE THE UNIT OR LESSON	AFTER THE UNIT OR LESSON
Feelings about it		
Thoughts about it		
Associations with it		
Mental images/pictures		

How am I different as a result of this unit or lesson?

Models for Student Journals

Note: Journals can involve different modes of reflecting including writing, drawing, painting, sculpting, role playing, dancing, etc.

CHART YOUR MOODS (to process feelings about a period/day)

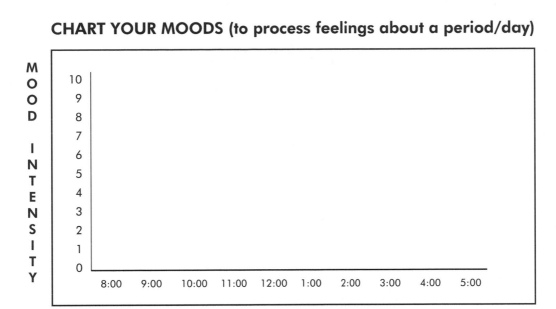

M O O D   I N T E N S I T Y

10
9
8
7
6
5
4
3
2
1
0

8:00   9:00   10:00   11:00   12:00   1:00   2:00   3:00   4:00   5:00

T I M E   S E Q U E N C E

1. At the end of the day plot your different moods of the day on the graph above. (The vertical numbers represent mood intensity and the horizontal numbers time sequences.)

2. Place a mark at the high point of the day and one at the low point. Then look at the time before and after these points; think about other changes in mood. Make marks at the appropriate places.

3. Now connect the marks with a continuous curving line so that you have a visual picture of the mood changes and the affective flow of the day.

4. For each point that you have marked along the axes, jot a brief note about what was going on that catalyzed the mood shift.

5. Using colored markers or crayons, create a spectrum of colors from left to right to match the different moods you experienced.

6. Finally, think of the kind of music you would play as a background for each of the different moods of the day. Note these on the graph.

7. Try doing this every day for a week. At the end of the week lay all of your mood graphs side by side and reflect on the week. What do you learn about yourself as you look at the week in this way?

Models for Student Journals

Note: Journals can involve different modes of reflecting including writing, drawing, painting, sculpting, role playing, dancing, etc.

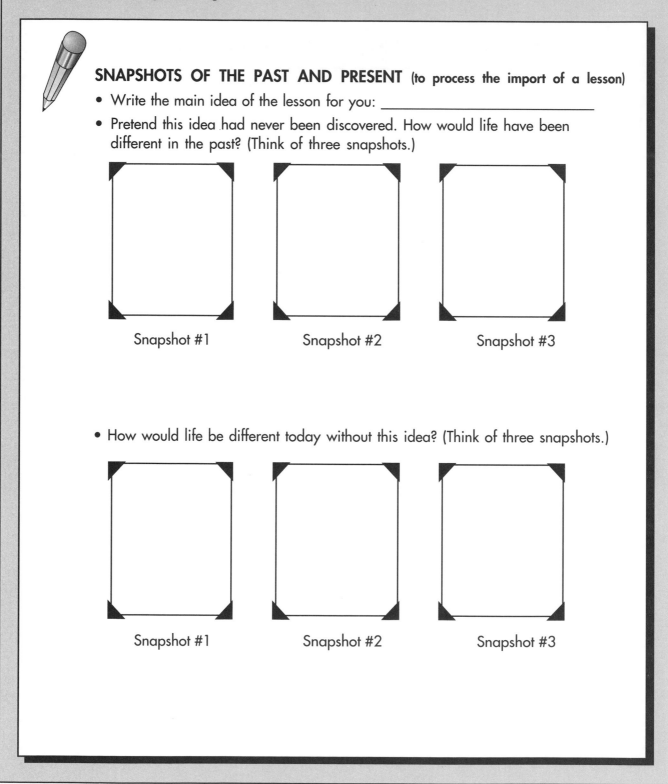

SNAPSHOTS OF THE PAST AND PRESENT (to process the import of a lesson)

- Write the main idea of the lesson for you: _____
- Pretend this idea had never been discovered. How would life have been different in the past? (Think of three snapshots.)

Snapshot #1   Snapshot #2   Snapshot #3

- How would life be different today without this idea? (Think of three snapshots.)

Snapshot #1   Snapshot #2   Snapshot #3

Models for Student Journals

Note: Journals can involve different modes of reflecting including writing, drawing, painting, sculpting, role playing, dancing, etc.

STEPPING STONES INTO THE FUTURE (to project future applications of a lesson)

- Write the main idea of the lesson for you: _____
- Brainstorm five ways this idea has been or is being applied in our times.

  1.

  2.

  3.

  4.

  5.

- Pretend you can step into the next century. How will this idea be applied then?

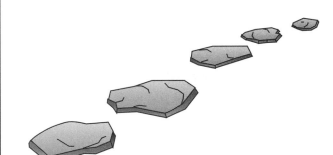

Key Ingredients for Success in Cooperative Learning

1. You must consciously bring **higher-order thinking** and reasoning to a lesson. Students must be taught how to think at higher levels and have lessons that challenge them to perform at these higher levels.

2. You must have a kit of strategies to **unify the teams.** You want to create a sense of "We need each other for this lesson" or what Roger and David Johnson call positive interdependence.

3. You must structure the lesson to **insure individual learning.** There should be no sloughing off on the part of the individuals just because they are in a group.

4. You must provide students enough time to **look over and discuss** both the lesson content and their cooperative behavior. As students process their lessons they become more and more aware that they are the key to their own educational success.

5. You must carefully and explicitly **develop the necessary social skills**—the necessary skills of effective cooperation and collaboration with others. These skills include such things as listening, encouraging, taking turns, staying on task, using appropriate voice volume, etc.

Note: This blackline is provided for teacher use when teaching cooperative lessons.

Eight Ways of Teaching Weekly Checklist

Have I taught for the eight ways of knowing this week? Check yourself by listing the specific strategies, techniques, and tools you have used in classroom lessons this week.

	MONDAY	TUESDAY	WEDNESDAY	THURSDAY	FRIDAY
Verbal/Linguistic					
Logical/Mathematical					
Visual/Spatial					
Bodily/Kinesthetic					
Musical/Rhythmic					
Interpersonal					
Intrapersonal					
Naturalist					

Note: This blackline is provided as a useful tool for teachers to think through their weekly multiple intelligences strategies.

LESSON PROCEDURE BLACKLINES

APPENDIX

B

SkyLight Training and Publishing Inc.

The 6 Ss for Describing Attributes

Object: _____

Sight _____

Sound _____

Smell _____

Sense (tactile)

Size _____

Speciality

Write 3 sentences telling different things about the object you find interesting

1.

2.

3.

See/Feel T-Chart

Object _____

What I See 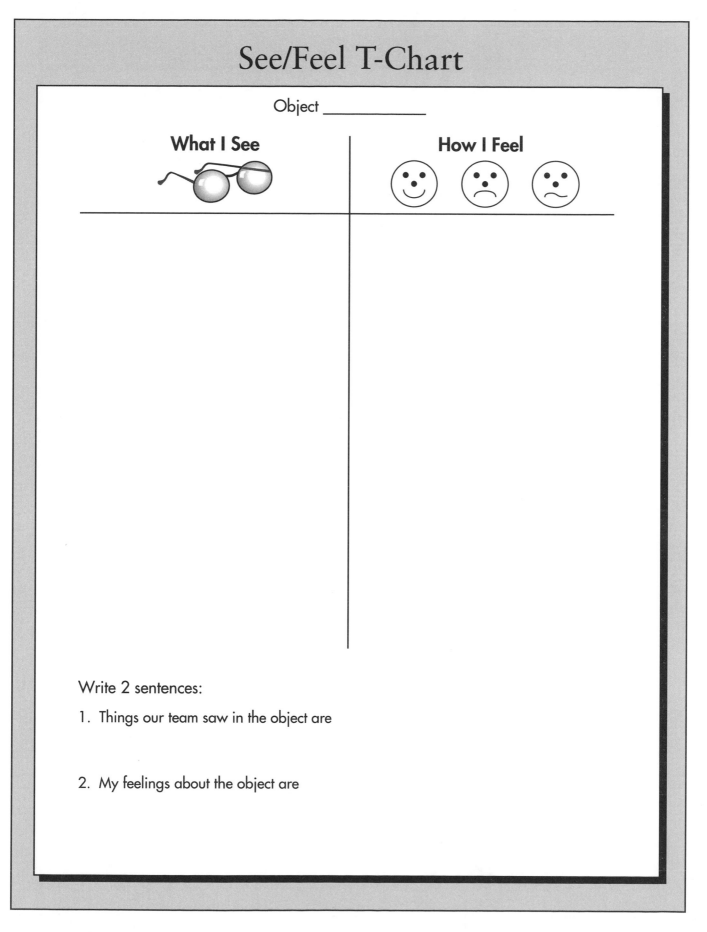	**How I Feel**

Write 2 sentences:

1. Things our team saw in the object are

2. My feelings about the object are

3 Graphic Organizers

Attribute Web

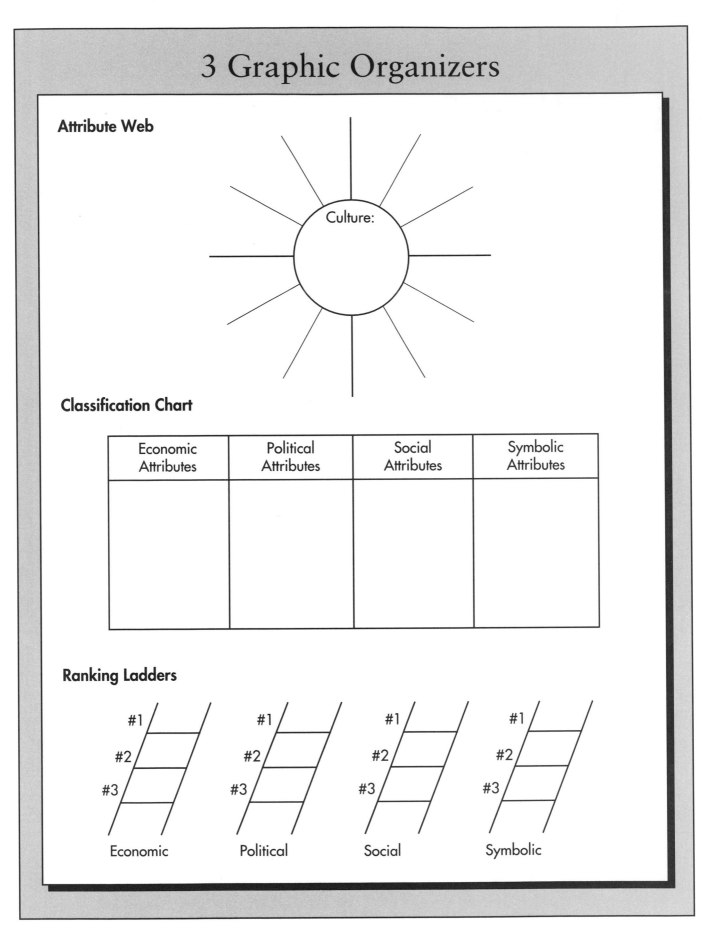

Culture:

Classification Chart

Economic Attributes	Political Attributes	Social Attributes	Symbolic Attributes

Ranking Ladders

#1
#2
#3
Economic

#1
#2
#3
Political

#1
#2
#3
Social

#1
#2
#3
Symbolic

How to Make Food from Sunlight
The Amazing Process of Photosynthesis

The wonders of photosynthesis have intrigued scientists ever since the phenomenon was first recognized. The overall process—the conversion of water and carbon dioxide into sugar—has been known for more than a century. While there are still many gaps in our understanding of photosynthesis, our information is growing.

Three outside ingredients are involved to get the whole process started: (1) water, which is drawn up into the plant through its roots and stems, (2) carbon dioxide, which enters the plant through pores on its many leaves, and (3) sunlight, which is the energy source that catalyzes the whole process.

The heart of the process lies in the chloroplasts, with their light-reacting pigment. The cells of the leaf are dotted with green chloroplasts. They are shaped like tiny footballs and can turn, within the cell, to take best advantage of the light, almost like a light-sensitive radar system. The chloroplasts are stacked on top of one another and are layered with chlorophyll molecules. The chlorophyll starts soaking up or absorbing the sunlight once the chloroplasts have located it. This absorption of light energy from the sun activates or turns on the chlorophyll. The chlorophyll splits the water molecule, producing hydrogen and oxygen. The oxygen is released into the air through the pores of the leaves. The hydrogen is instantly seized by a special escort molecule and will play an important role in the next step of the process.

Meanwhile, the chlorophyll molecule starts to deactivate and return to its normal state. As this happens, further energy is released which is used to create an energy-driver molecule called ATP (adenosine triphosphate) from certain materials already present in the plant. ATP is an energy unit that is present in all living organisms. It has the ability to supply energy to chemical reactions without itself becoming a part of the end product. This concludes the *photo* or the light-requiring part of the photosynthesis process.

The work of the chlorophyll is finished and the *synthesis* part begins. The carbon dioxide now lines up with an acceptor module that is already in the plant. This sets the stage for a critical union to occur. The hydrogen atom, led by its escort module and powered by ATP, combines with the carbon dioxide to form a highly reactive compound called PGA (phosphoglyceric acid). The PGA molecules then combine to form sugar, which in turn is stored in the plant for food.

The machinery for this process is very complex and the whole process happens almost instantaneously; but with the electron microscope, much of it can actually be seen.

Discussion Questions
for How to Make Food from Sunlight

1. What do you remember from the reading?

2. What was surprising to you? exciting? amazing?

3. Recall and list the stages of photosynthesis. What happens first, second, third, etc?

4. If you could have a conversation with a plant, what questions would you ask?

Physical Movement Formulas

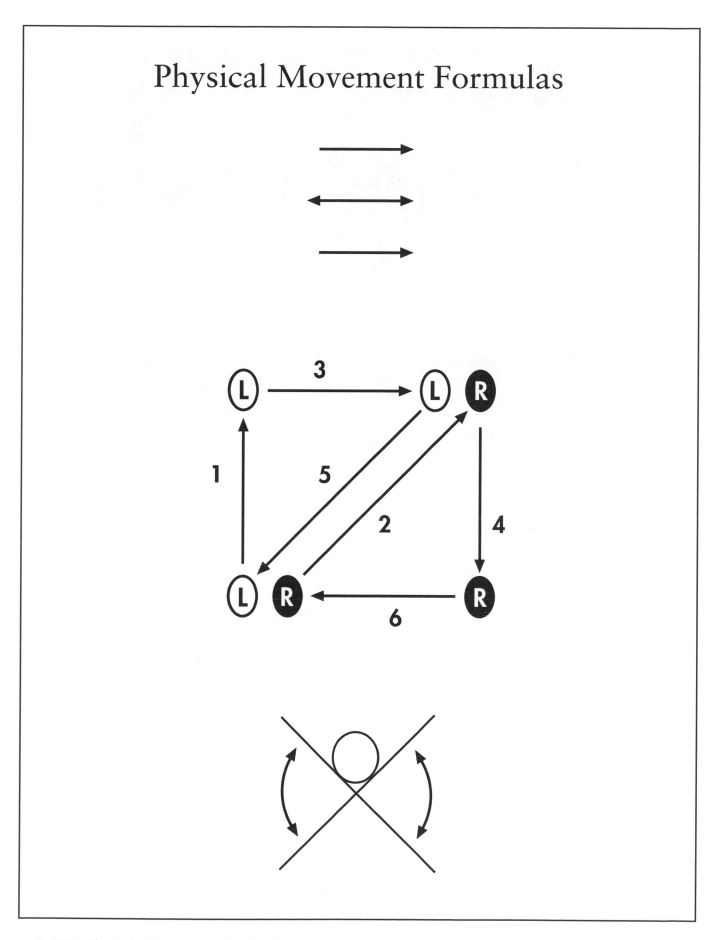

Fold into a tent card

In 1776, America signed the Declaration of Independence. In the Declaration, America says that it is breaking away from England and will be a nation on its own. The Declaration lists the reasons the Americans decided to become their own nation.

Thomas Jefferson wrote the Declaration of Independence. John Hancock was the first person to sign it. Then fifty-seven others also signed it to show their support for the move to become free from England.

Questions:
1. What is the Declaration of Independence about?

2. Who was its author?

3. How many people signed it?

4. Why did they sign it?

Team Reflection Log

	Show #1	Show #2	Show #3	Show #4
What was the story being told?				
How did it make you feel?				
What are your questions about this event?				
Why is this story important for us today?				

4-Level Reflection Model

LEVEL **1** HOW AM I INVOLVED?	Where and how does the issue touch my life? How does it make me feel? What are my thoughts and opinions about it?

LEVEL **2** WHAT ARE THE PLUSES, MINUSES, AND WHAT DO I FIND INTERESTING?	**Positive Aspects +**	**Negative Aspects −**	**Interesting I**

LEVEL **3** WHAT DO I THINK COULD OR SHOULD BE DONE?	If I was in charge what would I do? What do I think needs to happen in this situation? What action(s) should be taken?

LEVEL **4** WHAT CAN I DO NOW?	What steps could I take now (even small ones) to bring about a resolution to this issue?

Types of Writing Worksheet

	Declarative Writing statement expressing a simple fact *I'll meet you at the corner cafe.*	Interrogative Writing statement expressing a question *Should we meet at the cafe or elsewhere?*	Imperative Writing statement expressing a command *Be at the cafe no later than 11 a.m.*	Exclamatory Writing statement expressing a strong emphasis *We had a fabulous time at the cafe!*
The Sense of Smell *What odors are you aware of?*				
The Sense of Touch *What textures do you see and/or actually feel?*				
The Sense of Sight *What is catching the attention of your eyes?*				
The Sense of Hearing *What sounds are you hearing? Listen beyond the obvious—now what do you hear?*				
The Sense of Taste *What are you tasting in your mouth?*				
Inner Feelings and Thoughts *What are you feeling and/or thinking deep inside?*				

GRAPHIC ORGANIZER
BLACKLINES

APPENDIX

C

CONCEPT MAP

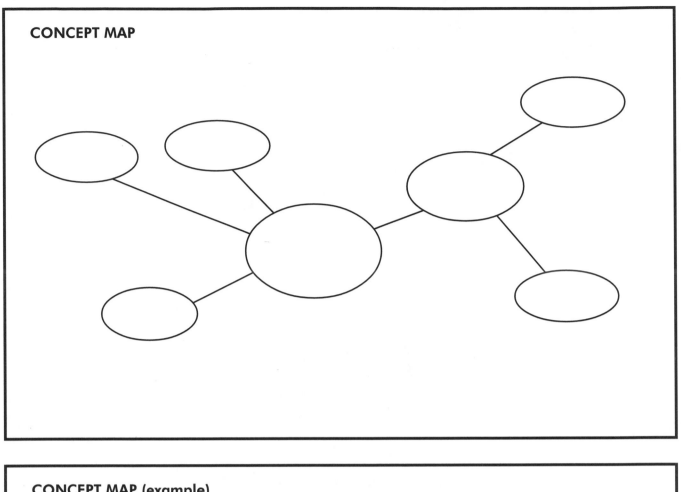

CONCEPT MAP (example)

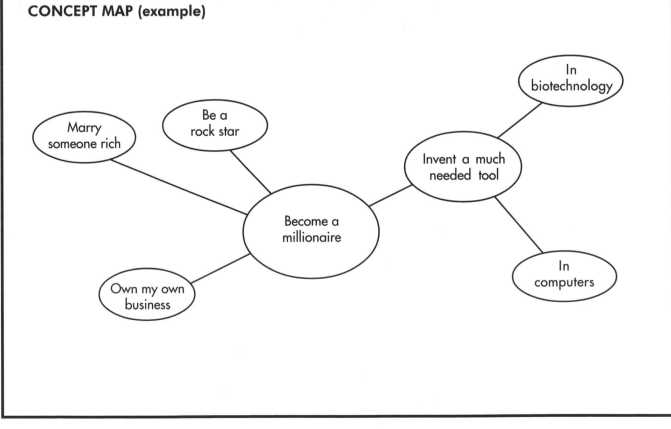

FAT AND SKINNY QUESTIONS

FAT	SKINNY
1.	1.
2.	2.
3.	3.
4.	4.
5.	5.

FAT AND SKINNY QUESTIONS (example)

FAT (requires discussion)	SKINNY (can be answered with one word)
1. Why did the colonists break away from England?	1. Who drafted the Declaration of Independence?
2. What would things be like if America were still a British colony?	2. Was George Washington involved in drafting the Declaration of Independence?
3.	3.
4.	4.
5.	5.

4 x 4 x 4 OUTLINE

I		II		III		IV	
A	1	A	1	A	1	A	1
	2		2		2		2
	3		3		3		3
	4		4		4		4
B	1	B	1	B	1	B	1
	2		2		2		2
	3		3		3		3
	4		4		4		4
C	1	C	1	C	1	C	1
	2		2		2		2
	3		3		3		3
	4		4		4		4
D	1	D	1	D	1	D	1
	2		2		2		2
	3		3		3		3
	4		4		4		4

4 x 4 x 4 (example)

On What Do I Spend My Time?

I Home		II Work		III Family		IV Self	
A The house	1 painting	A lesson planning	1 outline	A spouse	1 alone time	A reading	1 Harper's
	2 cleaning		2 research		2 help with bills		2 Moby Dick
	3 repairs		3 supplies		3 help with kids		3 newspaper
	4 bills		4 special activities		4 drive to activities		4 trade journals
B The garden	1 mowing	B grading	1 reading papers	B kids	1 drive to activities	B exercise	1 walking
	2 weeding		2 marking papers		2 cook for		2 swimming
	3 watering		3 tabulating grades		3 buy clothes		3 biking
	4 raking		4 recording grades		4 help with homework		4 bowling
C The pets	1 feeding	C teaching	1 attendance	C parents	1 talk on phone	C relaxation	1 watching television
	2 brushing		2 focusing		2 bring groceries		2 going to movies
	3 cleaning up		3 assignment		3 take kids to visit		3 sleeping
	4 taking to vet		4 monitoring		4 bring dinner		4 listening to music
D The car	1 repairs	D faculty meetings	1 preparing for	D church	1 attend Sunday	D seeing friends	1 dinner with Sue
	2 washing		2 sitting in		2 choir		2 movie with Gail
	3 filling with gas		3 taking notes		3 volunteer work		3 party at Bob's
	4 tuning up		4 discussing		4 usher		4 bridge club

JIGSAW

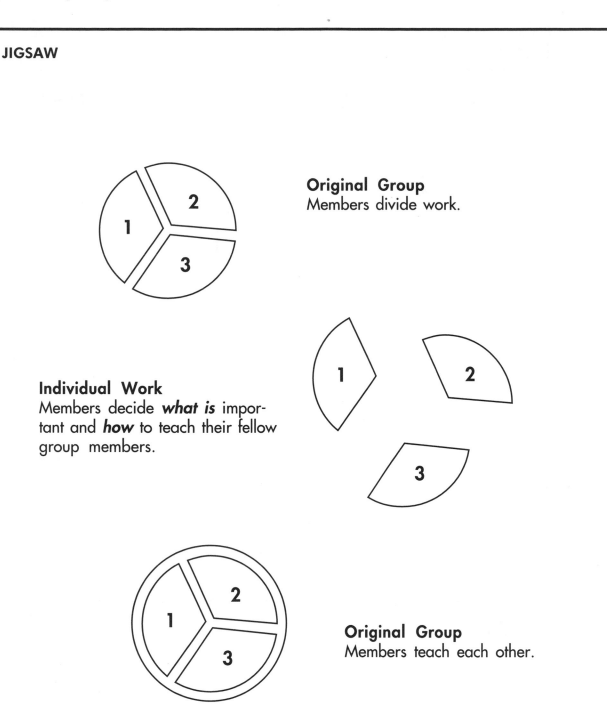

Original Group
Members divide work.

Individual Work
Members decide *what is* important and *how* to teach their fellow
group members.

Original Group
Members teach each other.

TWO DECISIONS

#1 What to teach

#2 How to teach it

KWL GOAL-SETTING CHART

What We **Know**	What We **Want** to Find Out	What We **Learned**

KWL CHART (example)

What We **Know**	What We **Want** to Find Out	What We **Learned**
There are different parts of speech.	How to correctly use each part of speech in sentences.	Parts of speech are like a paint palette from which you can create interesting sentences.

MATRIX

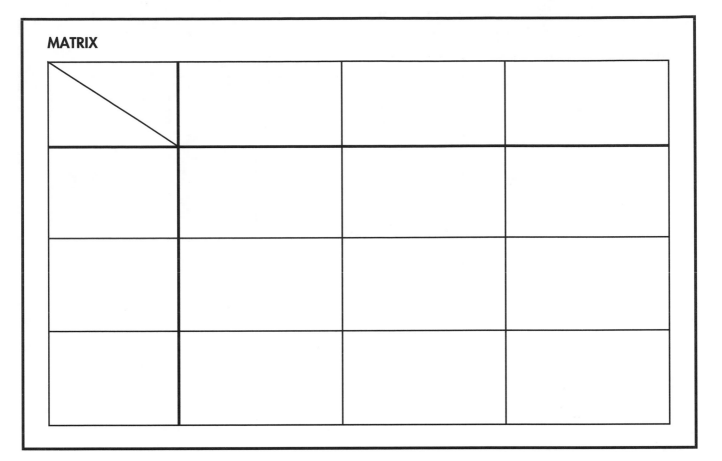

MATRIX (example)

GLOBAL ISSUE / COUNTRY	ENVIRONMENTAL CONCERN	HUMAN RIGHTS	CULTURAL DIVERSITY
MEXICO	Air Pollution	Homelessness	Indians
INDIA	Food Supply	Overpopulation	Religion
CANADA	Deforestation	Socialized Medicine	Language (French and English)

PMI CHART

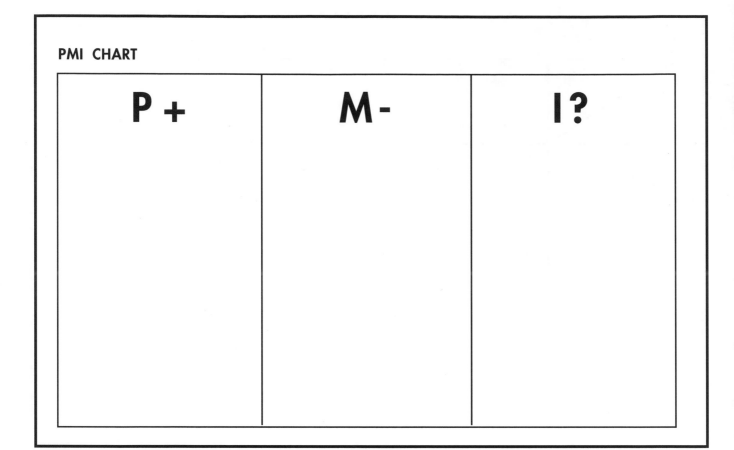

P +	M -	I ?

PMI CHART (example)   **Daughter's College Education**

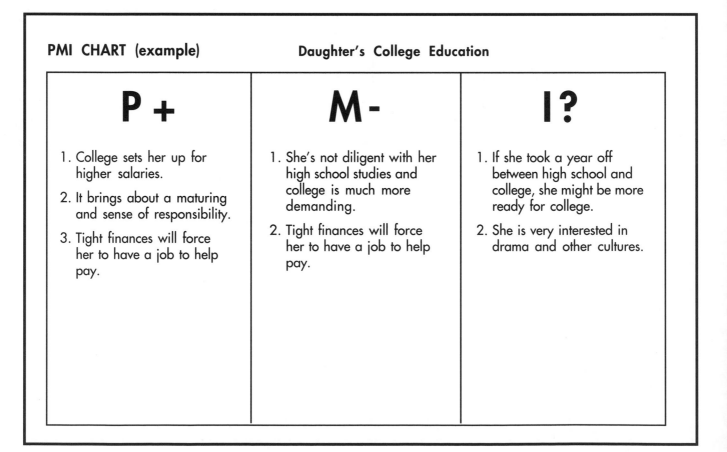

P +	M -	I ?
1. College sets her up for higher salaries. 2. It brings about a maturing and sense of responsibility. 3. Tight finances will force her to have a job to help pay.	1. She's not diligent with her high school studies and college is much more demanding. 2. Tight finances will force her to have a job to help pay.	1. If she took a year off between high school and college, she might be more ready for college. 2. She is very interested in drama and other cultures.

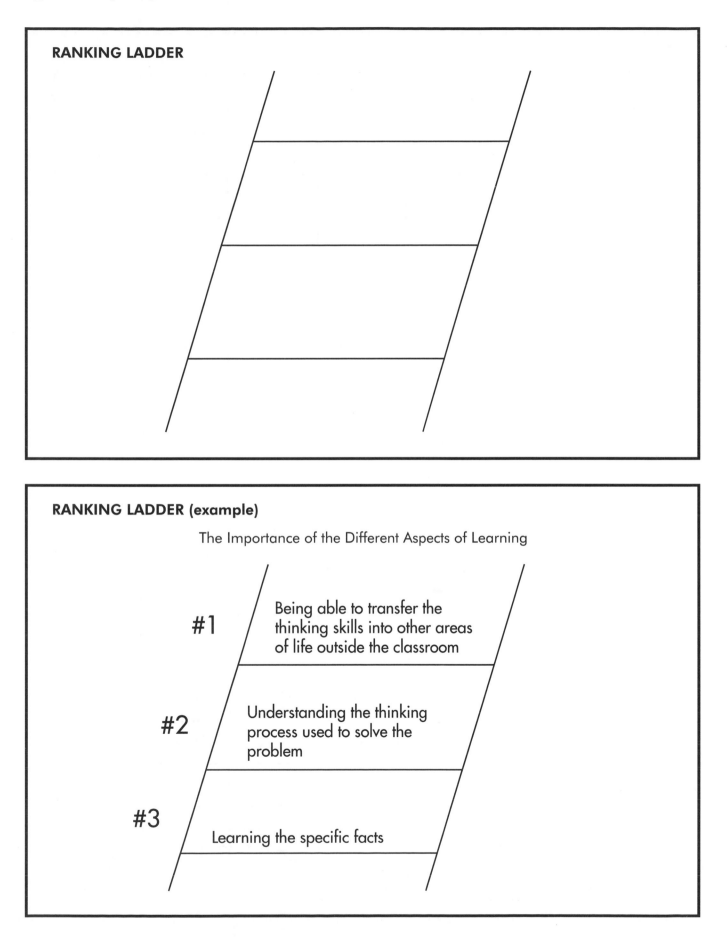

RANKING LADDER

RANKING LADDER (example)

The Importance of the Different Aspects of Learning

#1 Being able to transfer the thinking skills into other areas of life outside the classroom

#2 Understanding the thinking process used to solve the problem

#3 Learning the specific facts

STORY GRID

STORY GRID (example)

GOOD GUY	SIDEKICK	BAD GUY	GAL	CONFLICT	SETTING	ENDING
doctor	small boy	city slicker	lawyer	man vs. nature	1800s	cliff-hanger
lawyer	farmer	land baron	gambler	ranchers vs. farmers	closet	everyone happy
Indian chief	deputy	bully	schoolteacher	town vs. stranger	Montana	serial
marshal	relative	ex-con	widow	large bank deposit lost	town	tragic
stranger	friend	gambler	little kid	man vs. self	desert	butler did it
bartender	a dog	politician	eastern cousin	good vs. evil	saloon	bad guy wins
shop owner	rancher	lawyer	bank clerk	cowboys vs. Indians	mountain	everyone dies

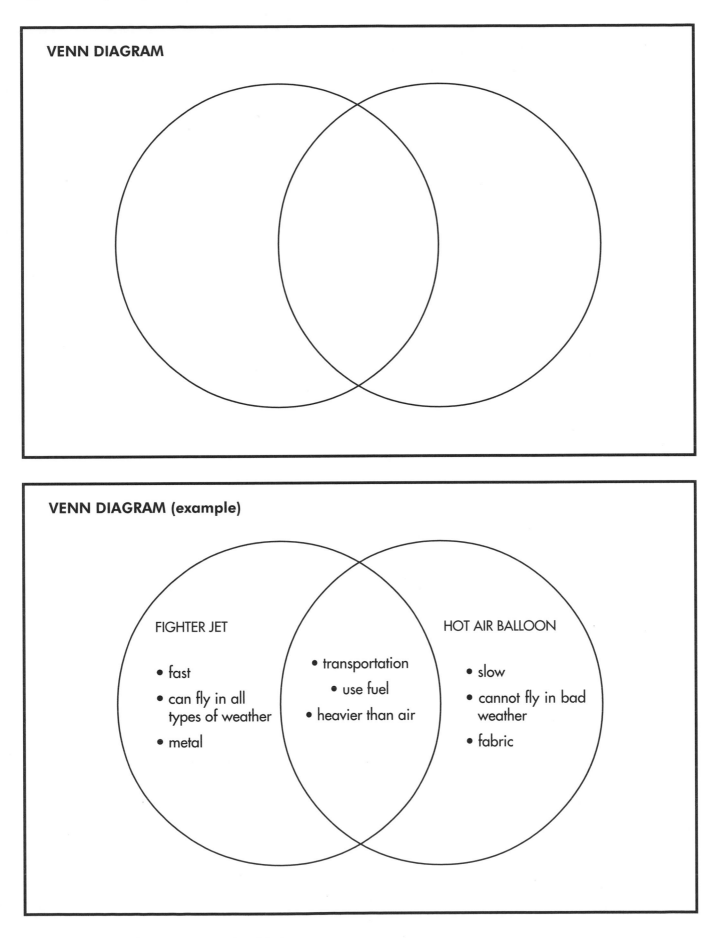

VENN DIAGRAM

VENN DIAGRAM (example)

FIGHTER JET

- fast
- can fly in all types of weather
- metal

- transportation
- use fuel
- heavier than air

HOT AIR BALLOON

- slow
- cannot fly in bad weather
- fabric

WEB

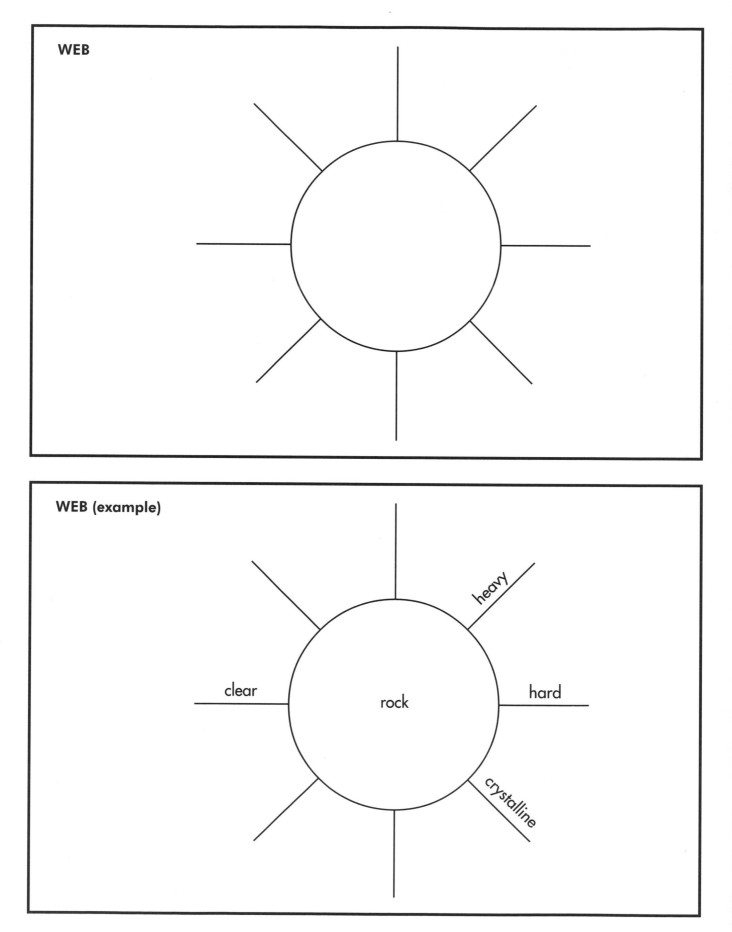

WEB (example)

clear

rock

heavy

hard

crystalline

WHAT? SO WHAT? NOW WHAT?

What? (What have I learned?)

So What? (What difference does it make?)

Now What? (What can I do with this information?)

WHAT? SO WHAT? NOW WHAT? (example)

What? (What have I learned?)

Oak is harder than pine.

So What? (What difference does it make?)

Oak will burn slower than the pine will.

Now What? (What can I do with this information?)

If I want my campfire to last longer, I will use oak instead of pine.

GLOSSARY

Glossary

amplify to expand, strengthen, and enhance one's intelligence capacities.

archetypal pattern recognition awareness of the many repeating and standard patterns and designs of nature which manifest themselves throughout the entire universe. *see also micro/macro pattern connections.*

attribute webbing a thinking strategy that involves brainstorming attributes or characteristics of something using the web graphic organizer (see blackline, p. 158).

awaken to trigger, catalyze, or assess latent intelligence capacities in the brain using specifically targeted exercises.

awareness technique any method or tool that gives one a new perspective, expands one's thinking horizons, or alters one's self-understanding.

biofeedback a technique for learning to control certain involuntary functions such as blood pressure, body temperature, heart rate, etc.

blackline a master copy from which photocopy reproductions can be made.

brainstorm to generate as many ideas as possible on a topic without evaluating or judging those ideas.

Broca's area the area of the brain, located in the front part of the left hemisphere, that is primarily responsible for the production and understanding of language.

caring for animals projects which involve caring for and/or training animals, insects, and other organisms

classification chart a graphic organizer that can help one learn the thinking skill of classifying things according to various criteria (see blackline, p. 158).

cognitive organizer a visual diagram of a thinking pattern or process.

concept mapping a thinking technique that begins with a central idea and proceeds to show related ideas as branches off of the center (see blackline, p. 168).

conservation practices participation in various projects to care for and preserve the natural environment including its animals.

countermelody a second melody in a song that is different from the main melody and yet fits perfectly with it when they are played simultaneously.

deep relaxation technique any method that assists one in achieving a more relaxed state of being.

dramatic structure model the classical structure of a Shakespeare play—action builds to a decisive climax followed by the results or implications of the climax.

Each One Teach One an interactive group strategy in which each person in a group learns something and then teaches it to the others in the group.

environmental feedback understanding and appreciating the environment by tuning in to the natural feedback coming from the environment.

fat and skinny questions a technique for helping students stimulate further thinking. Skinny questions can be answered with a yes or no. Fat questions require thoughtful creative responses (see blackline, p. 169).

focusing technique   any method or tool that helps one bring attention and thinking to a singular point.

4 x 4 x 4 outline   a graphic organizer that can help one learn how to organize thinking through main points, subpoints and sub-subpoints (see blackline, p. 170).

Gossip Game   a game in which something is whispered to the first person in a line of people and then is passed down the line in turn to each person, the point being to note how the final message has changed in the process.

graphic organizer   *see cognitive organizer.*

growing natural things   projects which involve growing and caring for plants, crystals, bacteria, etc.

guided imagery   a thinking process that activates one's imagination and capacity to pretend.

hands-on labs   performing experiments or activities which involve and utilize objects from the natural world.

How I Say *What* I Say   a verbal exercise in which the intended meaning of something is altered simply by the inflection, tone, and pitch of one's voice.

human graph   a thinking strategy that asks people to physically stand along a spectrum that indicates how they feel or think about an issue.

human sculpture tableau   the physical arrangement of a group of people such that postures and positions "embody" a certain idea or feeling.

I Become What I Behold   an empathy exercise that involves imagining that one can become another person, animal, or thing and, from that perspective, look back and observe the self.

inner seeing exercises   *see guided imagery.*

jigsaw   a cooperative learning strategy that involves giving each person in a group a portion of the whole to learn and then teach it to the others in the group (see blackline, p. 171).

KWL goal setting chart   a graphic organizer that helps one assess prior knowledge and current questions for a learning task, and then to assess what was actually learned after the task is completed (see blackline, p. 172).

live painting   *see human sculpture tableau.*

matrix   a way of classifying things on a chart with certain categories across the top and others down the side of the chart; items in the chart must meet the criteria of both the top and side category (see blackline, p. 173).

metacognition   the process of thinking about and analyzing one's own thinking processes.

metacognitive processing   the evaluation of one's own thinking after the completion of a learning activity.

micro/macro pattern connections   identifying similar patterns, shapes, designs, characteristics, etc., between differing layers of the planet's ecosystem (subatomic to universe).

mind map   same as concept map except it primarily uses pictures, images, colors, designs, and patterns to express concepts or ideas.

multitracking   any physical exercise that involves performing several different actions simultaneously (e.g., rubbing the stomach and patting the top of the head while jogging in place).

natural pattern recognition   identifying distinct patterns, designs, shapes, colors, etc., that belong to distinct environments or species (organic and inorganic).

nature encounters/field trips   going outside for firsthand experiences in nature and/or bringing nature in via videos, objects, animals, plants, etc.

nature observation   participation in activities such as bird-watching, noting geological differences, keeping nature journals, etc.

nature simulations   projects which re-create and/or represent nature in some form such as dioramas, montages, photographs, drawings, nature rubbings, etc.

New Word for the Day   a vocabulary expansion practice that involves learning the meaning of a new word each day and using it in conversation during the day.

noncompetitive game   a game in which the point is to have fun playing, not defeating the opponent.

pass over   *see I Become What I Behold.*

peer coaching team   a cooperative group in which the members have agreed to help each other improve certain skills by giving each other positive feedback and advice.

PMI   a graphic organizer that helps one learn the thinking skill of evaluation (P = pluses, M = minuses, I = interesting) (see blackline, p. 174).

ranking ladder   a graphic organizer that helps one learn the thinking skill of prioritizing (see blackline, p. 175).

rhythm game   a game that involves recalling certain numbers and number patterns to rhythmic hand clapping and finger snapping.

sensory stimulation exercises   sensory-based exposure to and participation in nature's sounds, smells, tastes, touches, and sights.

species classification (organic/inorganic)   working with classification matrices to understand characteristics of natural objects.

species discrimination   recognizing and understanding basic and complex similarities and differences between distinguishing characteristics of different species.

spiral adaptation   altering a particular lesson so it is appropriate for different grade levels or age groups.

Stop the Action and Improvise   a drama technique in which actors play a scene and the director stops the action at a random point and asks the actors to improvise the rest of the scene.

story grid   a graphic organizer that contains basic information for a story (e.g. hero, heroine, villain, setting, conflict, ending) that is randomly chosen and woven together to create a final story (see blackline, p. 176).

transfer   the process of making connections between one's learning and daily life.

Turn to Your Partner And . . .   an interactive strategy in which two people who are seated next to each other discuss and/or process information, share feelings and thoughts, and explore ideas.

ugly Americanism   rude and insensitive behavior of American tourists visiting other cultures.

Venn diagram   a graphic organizer in which two or more overlapping circles help teach the thinking skill of comparing and contrasting (see blackline, p. 177).

web   a graphic organizer that helps one learn the thinking skill of brainstorming (see blackline, p. 178).

What? So What? Now What?   a processing technique used after one has acquired some new information. The technique uses these questions: What have I learned? So what difference does it make? Now what can I do with this information? (see blackline, p. 179).

SkyLight Training and Publishing Inc.

BIBLIOGRAPHY

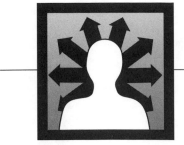

Bibliography

Alexander, F. 1984. *The use of the self: Its conscious direction in relation to diagnosis, functioning, and the control of reaction.* Downey, Calif.: Centerline Press.

Ambruster, B., and T. Anderson. 1980. *The effect of mapping on the free recall of expository tests. Tech. Rep. No. 160.* Urbana-Champaign, IL: University of Illinois, Center for the Study of Reading.

Anderson, R., and W. Biddle. 1975. On asking people questions about what they are reading. In *The psychology of learning and motivation,* edited by G. Bower. New York: Academic Press.

Arlin, P. 1990. Teaching as conversation. *Educational Leadership* 48(2).

Armstrong, T. 1987. *In their own way: Discovering and encouraging your child's personal learning style.* Los Angeles: J.P. Tarcher.

Assagioli, R. 1973. *The act of will.* New York: Viking Press.

Ausubel, D. 1968. *Educational psychology: A cognitive view.* New York: Holt, Rinehart, and Winston.

Bacon, F. 1939. Of studies. In *Century readings in the English essay,* edited by W. Louis. New York: Appleton-Century-Crofts.

Bartlett, F. 1958. *Thinking.* New York: Basic Books.

Bellanca, J., and R. Fogarty. 1991. *Blueprints for thinking in the cooperative classroom* (rev. ed.). Arlington Heights, Ill.: IRI/ SkyLight Training and Publishing.

Bellanca, J., and R. Fogarty. 1986. *Catch them thinking.* Arlington Heights, Ill.: IRI/SkyLight Training and Publishing.

Benson, H. 1975. *The relaxation response.* New York: Morrow.

Berlin, B. 1992. *Ethnobiological classification: Principles of categorization of plants and animals in traditional societies.* Princeton, N.J.: Princeton University Press.

Beyer, B. 1987. *Practical strategies for the teaching of thinking.* Boston: Allyn & Bacon.

Bloom, B. 1956. *Taxonomy of educational objectives.* New York: David McKay.

Bogen, J. 1979. Some educational aspects of hemispheric socialization. *Dromenon* (February).

Boulding, K. 1966. *The image.* Ann Arbor: University of Michigan Press.

Bruner, J., J. Goodnow, and G. Austin. 1956. *A study of thinking.* New York: Wiley.

Buzan, T. 1991. *Use both sides of your brain.* New York: Dutton.

Caine, R., and G. Caine. 1990. Understanding a brain-based approach to learning and teaching. *Educational Leadership* 48(2): 66–70.

Campbell, D. 1983. *Introduction to the musical brain.* Richardson, Tex.: Magnamusic-Baton.

Campbell, J. 1989. *The improbable machine: What the upheavals in artificial intelligence research reveal about how the mind really works.* New York: Simon and Schuster.

Campbell, L. 1985. *Tomorrow's education today.* Seattle: The Pegasus School.

Caramassa, A., A. Hillis, E. C. Leek, and M. Miozzo. 1994. The organization of lexical knowledge in the brain: Evidence from category- and modality-specific deficits. In *Mapping the mind,* edited by L. Hirschfield and S. Gelman. New York: Cambridge University Press.

Carey, S. 1985. *Conceptual change in childhood.* Cambridge, Mass.: MIT Press.

Chi, M. 1981. Knowledge development and memory performance. In *Intelligence and learning,* edited by M. Friedman, J. P. Das, and N. O'Connor. New York: Plenum.

Chomsky, N. 1968. *Language and mind.* New York: Harcourt, Brace, Jovanovich.

Coles, R. 1990. *The spiritual life of children.* Boston: Houghton Mifflin.

Costa, A., ed. 1991. *Developing minds* (rev. ed.). Alexandria, Va.: Association for Supervision and Curriculum Development.

Costa, A. 1991. The school as a home for the mind. In *Developing Minds, Volume 1* (rev. ed.), edited by A. Costa. Alexandria, Va.: Association for Supervision and Curriculum Development.

Costa, A. 1984. Mediating the metacognitive. *Educational Leadership* (42)3: 57–62.

Costa, A. 1981. Teaching for intelligent behavior. *Educational Leadership* (39)1: 29–31.

Csikszentmihalyi, N. 1996. *Creativity.* New York: Harper Collins.

Culicover, P. and P. Wexler. 1980. *Formal principles of language acquisition.* Cambridge, Mass.: MIT Press.

Curry, L. 1990. A critique of the research on learning styles. *Educational Leadership* (48)2: 50–52.

Damasio, A. 1994. *Descartes's error.* New York: Putnam.

Dansereau, D., et al. 1979. Development and evaluation of a learning strategy training program. *Journal of Educational Psychology* 71(1).

Davidson, J. 1982. The group mapping activity for instruction in reading and thinking. *Journal of Reading* 26(1): 52–56.

de Bono, E. 1973. *Lateral thinking: Creativity step by step.* New York: Harper & Row.

Demille, R. 1976. *Put your mother on the ceiling.* New York: Viking-Penguin.

Dickinson, D. 1987. *New developments in cognitive research.* Seattle: New Horizons for Learning.

Dunne, J. 1972. *The way of all the earth: Experiments in truth and religion.* New York: MacMillan.

Edelman, G. M. 1995. *The wordless metaphor: Visual art and the brain.* New York: Witney Museum.

Feldenkrais, M. 1977. *Awareness through movement: Health exercises for personal growth.* New York: Harper and Row.

Ferguson, M. 1980. *The Aquarian conspiracy: Personal and social transformation in the 1980s.* Los Angeles: J. P. Tarcher.

Feuerstein, R. 1980. *Instrumental enrichment.* Baltimore, Md.: University Park Press.

Fogarty, R., and J. Bellanca. 1989. *Patterns for thinking: Patterns for transfer.* Arlington Heights, IL: IRI/SkyLight Training and Publishing.

Fogarty, R., and J. Bellanca. 1986. *Teach them thinking.* Arlington Heights, IL: IRI/SkyLight Training and Publishing.

Gardner, H. 1996. Are there additional intelligences? Cambridge, Mass.: Harvard Graduate School of Education.

Gardner, H. 1987. Developing the spectrum of human intelligences: Teaching in the eighties, a need to change. *Harvard Educational Review.*

Gardner, H. 1983. *Frames of mind: The theory of multiple intelligences.* New York: Harper and Row.

Gardner, H. 1982. *Developmental psychology: An introduction.* Boston: Little Brown.

Gardner, H. 1981. Do babies sing a universal song? *Psychology Today* (December).

Gawain, S. 1978. *Creative visualization.* New York: Bantam Books.

Gazzaniga, M. 1988. *Mind matters: How mind and brain interact to create our conscious lives.* Boston: Houghton Mifflin.

Gendlin, E. 1978. *Focusing.* New York: Everest House.

Glasser, W. 1986. *Control theory in the classroom.* New York: Perennial Library.

Graham, I. 1988. Mindmapping: An aid to memory. *Planetary Edges,* April/June. Toronto: The Institute of Cultural Affairs.

Gross, C. B. 1973. Visual functions of intero-temporal cortex. In *Handbook of sensory philosophy* (vol. II, no. 3), edited by R. Jung. New York: Springer Verlag.

Guilford, J. 1979. *Way beyond IQ.* Buffalo, N.Y.: Creative Education Foundation.

Harman, W. 1988. *The global mind change.* Indianapolis: Knowledge Systems.

Harman, W., and H. Rheingold. 1985. *Higher creativity.* Los Angeles: J. P. Tarcher.

Herrnstein, R. and D. Loveland. 1976. Natural concepts in pigeons. *Journal of Experimental Psychology: Animal Behavior Processes* 2:285–302.

Hoerr, T. 1996. *Succeeding with multiple intelligences.* St. Louis, Mo.: New City School.

Houston, J. 1987. *The search for the beloved: Journeys in sacred psychology.* Los Angeles: J. P. Tarcher.

Houston, J. 1982. *The possible human: A course in extending your physical, mental, and creative abilities.* Los Angeles: J. P. Tarcher.

Houston, J. 1980. *Lifeforce: The psycho-historical recovery of the self.* New York: Delacorte Press.

Hubbard, B. 1985. *Manual for co-creators of the quantum leap.* Irvine, Calif.: Barbara Mary Hubbard, Inc.

Institute of Cultural Affairs. 1981. Imaginal training methods. *Image: A Journal on the Human Factor.*

Institute of Cultural Affairs. 1968. *5th city preschool education manual.* Chicago: Institute of Cultural Affairs.

Johnson, D., R. Johnson, and E. J. Holubec. 1988. *Cooperation in the classroom.* Edina, Minn.: Interaction Book Company.

Johnson, D., R. Johnson, and E. J. Holubec. 1986. *Circles of learning.* Edina Minn.: Interaction Book Company.

Kagan, S. 1990. *Cooperative learning resources for teachers.* San Juan Capistrano, Calif.: Resources for Teachers.

Kazantzakis, N. 1960. *The saviors of god.* New York: Simon & Schuster.

Keil, F. 1994. The birth and nurturance of concepts by domains: The origins of concepts of living things. In *Mapping the mind,* edited by L. Hirschfield and S. A. Gelman. New York: Cambridge University Press.

Konorski, J. 1967. *Integrative activity of the brain: An interdisciplinary approach.* Chicago: University of Chicago Press.

Laird, C. 1957. *The miracle of language.* New York: Fawcett Publications.

Langer, S. 1979. *Reflections on art.* New York: Arno Press.

Lawrence, D. H. 1959. Search for love. In *The complete poems of D.H. Lawrence,* edited by V. de Sola Pinto and F. Roberts. New York: Viking Press.

Lazear, D. 1998. *Eight ways of knowing: Teaching for multiple intelligences* (3rd ed.). Arlington Heights, Ill.: IRI/SkyLight Training and Publishing.

Lazear, D. 1994. *Multiple intelligence approaches to assessment: Solving the assessment conundrum.* Tucson, Ariz.: Zephyr Press.

Lazear, D. 1994. *Seven pathways of learning: Teaching students and parents about multiple intelligences.* Tucson, Ariz.: Zephyr Press.

Lazear, D. 1996. *Step beyond your limits! Expanding your MI capacities.* Tucson, Ariz.: Zephyr Press.

Lederer, R. 1987. *Anguished English.* New York: Dell Publishing.

Loye, D. 1983. *The sphinx and the rainbow: Brain, mind, and future vision.* Boulder, Colo.: New Science Library.

Lozonov, G. 1978. *Suggestology and outlines of suggestology.* New York: Gordon & Breach.

Machado, L. 1980. *The right to be intelligent.* New York: Pergamon Press.

MacLean, P. 1977. On the evolution of three mentalities. In *New dimensions in psychiatry: A world view* (Vol. 2.), edited by S. Arieti and G. Chryanowski. New York: Wiley.

Markley, O. 1988. Using depth intuition in creative problem solving and strategic innovation. *Journal of Creative Behavior* (22)2: 85–100.

Martin, A., C. L. Wiggs, L. G. Ungerleider, and J. W. Haxby. 1996. Neural correlates of category-specific knowledge. *Nature* 376: 649–652.

Masters, R., and J. Houston. 1978. *Listening to the body: The psychophysical way to health and awareness.* New York: Delacorte Press.

Masters, R., and J. Houston. 1972. *Mind games.* New York: Delacorte Press.

McTighe, J. 1987. Teaching for thinking, of thinking, and about thinking. In *Thinking skills instruction: Concepts and techniques,* edited by M. Heiman and J. Slomianko. Washington, D.C.: National Education Association.

McTighe, J., and F. Lyman. 1988. Cueing thinking in the classroom: The promise of theory-embedded tools. *Educational Leadership* (45)7: 18–24.

Monroe, R. 1985. *Far journeys.* Garden City, N.Y.: Doubleday.

Nhat Hanh, T. 1988. *The miracle of mindfulness.* New York: Beacon Press.

Neisser, U. 1976. *Cognition and reality.* San Francisco: Freeman.

Nielsen, J. 1946. *Agnosia, apraxia, and aphasia: Their value in cerebral localization.* New York: Hoeber.

Orff, C. 1978. *The schoolwork.* Translated by M. Murray. New York: Schott Music Corporation.

Perkins, D. 1986. *Knowledge as design.* Hillsdale, N.J.: Lawrence Erlbaum Associates.

Piaget, J. 1972. *The psychology of intelligence.* Totowa, N.J.: Littlefield Adams.

Pribram, K. 1974. *Holonomy and structure in the organization of perception.* Stanford, Calif.: Stanford University Press.

Pribram, K. 1971. *Languages of the brain: Experimental paradoxes and principles in neuro-psychology.* Englewood Cliffs, N.J.: Prentice-Hall.

Progoff, I. 1975. *At a journal workshop: The basic text and guide for using the intensive journal.* New York: Dialogue House Library.

Rico, G. 1983. *Writing the natural way: Using right-brain techniques to release your expressive powers.* Los Angeles: J. P. Tarcher.

Roe, A. 1953. *The making of a scientist.* New York: Dodd, Mead.

Rosch, E., C. Mervis, W. Gray, D. Johnson, and P. Bayes-Braem. 1976. Basic objects in natural categories. *Cognitive Psychology* 8: 382–439.

Rosenfield, I. 1988. *The invention of memory: A new view of the brain.* New York: Basic Books.

Russell, P. 1983. *The global brain: Speculations on the evolutionary leap to planetary consciousness.* Los Angeles: J. P. Tarcher.

Russell, P. 1976. *The brain book.* New York: E.P. Dutton.

Samuels, M., and N. Samuels. 1975. *Seeing with the mind's eye: The history, techniques, and uses of visualization.* New York: Random House.

Schmeck, R. Ed. 1988. *Learning strategies and learning styles.* New York: Plenum Press.

Shone, R. 1984. *Creative visualization.* New York: Thorson's Publishers.

Slavin, R. 1983. *Cooperative learning.* New York: Longman.

Snowman, J. 1989. Learning tactics and strategies. In *Cognitive instructional psychology: Components of classroom learning,* edited by G. Phy and T. Andre. New York: Academic Press.

Springer, S., and G. Deutsch. 1985. *Left brain, right brain.* New York: W. H. Freeman.

Steiner, R. 1925. *Music in light of anthroposophy.* London: Anthroposophical.

Sternberg, R. 1986. *Intelligence applied: Understanding and increasing your intellectual skills.* San Diego, Calif.: Harcourt, Brace, Jovanovich.

Sternberg, R. 1984. *Beyond I.Q.: A triarchic theory of human intelligence.* New York: Cambridge University Press.

Sternberg, R., L. Okagaki, and A. Jackson. 1990. Practical intelligence for success in school. *Educational Leadership* (48)1: 35–39.

Striker, S. with E. Kimmel. 1982–1990. *The anti coloring book.* (Series.) New York: Holt.

Taylor, C., and F. Barron. 1963. *Scientific creativity, its recognition and development.* New York: Wiley.

Vaughn, F. 1986. *The inward arc.* Boulder, Colo.: The New Science Library.

von Oech, R. 1986. *A kick in the seat of the pants: Using your explorer, artist, judge, & warrior to be more creative.* New York: Perennial Library.

von Oech, R. 1983. *A whack on the side of the head: How to unlock your mind for innovation.* New York: Warner Books.

Vygotsky, L. 1986. *Thought and language.* Cambridge, Mass.: MIT Press.

Walsh, R., and F. Vaughn, eds. 1980. *Beyond ego: Transpersonal dimensions in psychology.* Los Angeles: J. P. Tarcher.

Walters, J., and H. Gardner. 1985. The development and education of the intelligences. *Essays on the Intellect.* Alexandria, Va.: Association for Supervision and Curriculum Development.

Warrington, E., and T. Shallice. 1984. Category-specific semantic impairments. *Brain* 107: 829–854.

Warrington, E. 1994. The conceptual abilities of pigeons. *American Scientist* 83: 246–255.

Weinstein, M., and J. Goodman. 1980. *Playfair.* San Luis Obispo, Calif.: Impact.

Wilber, K. 1983. *Eye to eye: The quest for the new paradigm.* Garden City, N.Y.: Anchor Books.

Wilber, K. 1980. *The atman project.* Wheaton, Ill.: Quest Books.

Winocur, S. L. 1986. Zooley. *IMPACT (improve minimal proficiency by activating critical thinking) program.* Huntington Beach, Calif.: Phi Delta Kappa.

INDEX

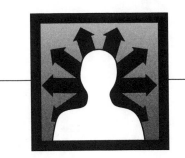

Index

SkyLight

PROFESSIONAL DEVELOPMENT

We Prepare Your Teachers Today
for the Classrooms of Tomorrow

Learn from Our Books and from Our Authors!

Ignite Learning in Your School or District.

SkyLight's team of classroom-experienced consultants can help you foster systemic change for increased student achievement.

Professional development is a process, not an event. SkyLight's experienced practitioners drive the creation of our on-site professional development programs, graduate courses, research-based publications, interactive video courses, teacher-friendly training materials, and online resources—call SkyLight Professional Development today.

SkyLight specializes in three professional development areas.

Specialty # 1 Best Practices

We **model** the best practices that result in improved student performance and guided applications.

Specialty # 2 Making the Innovations Last

We help set up **support** systems that make innovations part of everyday practice in the long-term systemic improvement of your school or district.

Specialty # 3 How to Assess the Results

We prepare your school leaders to encourage and **assess** teacher growth, **measure** student achievement, and **evaluate** program success.

Contact the SkyLight team and begin a process toward long-term results.

SkyLight
PROFESSIONAL DEVELOPMENT

2626 S. Clearbrook Dr., Arlington Heights, IL 60005
800-348-4474 • 847-290-6600 • 847-290-6609
info@skylightedu.com • www.skylightedu.com

There are
one-story intellects,
two-story intellects, and three-story
intellects with skylights. All fact collectors, who
have no aim beyond their facts, are one-story men. Two-story men
compare, reason, generalize, using the labors of the fact collectors as
well as their own. Three-story men idealize, imagine,
predict—their best illumination comes from
above, through the skylight.

—*Oliver Wendell*

Holmes

PROFESSIONAL DEVELOPMENT